ELIZABETH CRUZ

Foreword by: Dr. Matilde Castiel

ELLA PODEROSA

Poderosa voices, deeply rooted in strength, rising in unity, shaping our legacies and inspiring the next generation.

VOL. 1

ELLA Poderosa, Volume 1

This book is a compilation of stories from numerous Latinas who have each contributed a chapter and is designed to provide inspiration to our readers.

It is sold with the understanding that the publisher and the individual authors are not engaged in the rendering of psychological, legal, accounting or other professional advice. The content and views in each chapter are the sole expression and opinion of its author and not necessarily the views of Fig Factor Media, LLC.

For more information, contact:

Fig Factor Media, LLC | www.figfactormedia.com
Ella Poderosa | www.ella-ella.org

Cover Design by DG Marco Alvarez
Layout by LDG Juan Manuel Serna Rosales

Printed in the United States of America

ISBN: 978-1-961600-86-7
Library of Congress Control Number: 2025918222

To my mami, *mi Reina sin Corona*, whose quiet strength and unconditional love taught me that true leadership is lived through service, sacrifice, and gratitude.

To the *Poderosas* whose stories fill these pages—you are proof that resilience and courage cannot be silenced.

And to the next generation of *Latinas*—our daughters, nieces, and students—may this book remind you that you are never alone, and that the doors of leadership are open for you to walk through, with confidence and pride.

Table of Contents

Acknowledgments

No book is ever written alone. While the stories in these pages belong to each woman who had the courage to share her truth, the creation of this anthology has been a collective journey — one that I could not have walked without love, encouragement, and support.

First, to my husband and my son — thank you for being my constant source of strength, patience, and unconditional love. You have supported me through the long nights, the busy seasons, and the countless hours poured into making this dream a reality. Your belief in me reminds me daily that my work is never just mine — it is ours.

To the incredible Poderosas who contributed their stories: this book exists because of your bravery, your authenticity, and your willingness to open the door for others. Your words are a gift to our community and a legacy for the next generation.

To our publishing partners — thank you for your patience, professionalism, creativity, and care. You understood that this book is not just a publication, but a legacy of voices that deserve to be seen, honored, and amplified.

A special thank you to our editor, whose guidance, attention to detail, and belief in this project helped bring clarity and strength to every page.

To Dr. Matilde Castiel — thank you for gracing this anthology with your wisdom in the foreword. Your life's work embodies the same values of service, resilience, and compassion that live within these stories. Your words remind us that leadership is not just about position, but about heart.

To my partners, mentors, and mi queridas amigas who have stood beside me through the work of LABO and ELLA — thank you for reminding me that representation matters, that our voices matter, and that when one of us rises, we all rise.

To the Ruiz Family Foundation — thank you for your generous sponsorship and belief in ELLA Poderosa Volume 1. Your support made it possible to bring this vision to life, to open the door wider for Latina voices, and to help amplify the stories of leaders, entrepreneurs, and trailblazers whose resilience, leadership, and empowerment will inspire generations to come.

And above all, to every reader holding this book in your hands — thank you. By reading, reflecting, and sharing, you are part of this legacy. Together, we continue to build a future where Latinas do not just take up space, but create it.

Con gratitud,
Elizabeth Cruz, Founder & President
Empowering Latina Leaders Affirmation Inc (ELLA)

Foreword

I always begin with my background. Because our stories matter.

They are the heartbeat of our lives and the blueprint of our resilience. In telling mine, I hope you feel encouraged to share yours, because in those shared stories, we discover purpose, healing, and strength. That is how we fight inequity. That is how we push back against injustice, together.

So let me take you back.

I was seven years old. My brother was eight. We were Cuban immigrants, part of a quiet chapter in history known as Operation Peter Pan; a secret mission that brought over 14,000 children from Cuba to the United States without their parents. Our parents feared we'd be taken by the government. Indoctrinated. Silenced. So, they did the unthinkable; they let us go.

We left everything behind. Everyone.

On July 4, 1962, my mother packed one small suitcase with great care, tucking socks inside one another to make room for just a little more. At Havana's airport, my brother and I were placed in a glass enclosure called "The Fishbowl." We could see our parents, but we couldn't touch them. We kissed them goodbye through a pane of glass and stepped onto a plane into the unknown.

We arrived in Miami and were placed with a foster family. My first request? A visit to a grocery store. In Cuba, we waited in long lines for basic food. So, the idea that you could walk into a building and see rows of food just sitting there; it overwhelmed me.

Eventually, we were reunited with our parents. My father, with a third-grade education, stripped paint from furniture. My mother folded towels in a factory. They gave up everything so we could have something, a future.

For me, that future meant becoming a doctor.

But it didn't come easily.

My mother didn't believe medicine was a profession for women. My high school counselor told me I was a great typist; maybe I could be a secretary. Or, if I worked hard, perhaps a teacher.

But something inside me said: No, you don't get to define me. I will define myself.

So, I worked. I studied. I pushed through every door that tried to stay shut. I was admitted to UCSF Medical School. One of the best in the country, through affirmative action. A policy that no longer exists.

It wasn't always welcoming. Some said I didn't belong. That I took someone else's spot.

But I knew the truth: I earned my place.

When I walked across that stage to receive my diploma, I carried generations with me, my parents, that little girl behind glass, and every child who's ever been told their dreams were too big.

I came to Worcester to finish my residency. My husband and I had agreed we'd stay for two years.

That was thirty-six years ago.

I raised my children in Worcester. I'm now a proud grandmother. And through it all, my compass never changed; I was here to serve.

In 2004, I met a man named Hector Reyes. We heard rising concerns about violence in the Main South area, and saw addiction and homelessness being scapegoated. Together, we dreamed up a treatment facility for Latino men, culturally and linguistically appropriate. We had no experience. No money. I had never asked a bank for anything in my life, but Bay State Savings took a chance on us. We opened in 2009. Hector passed away just months later, but his legacy lives on. Today, the Hector Reyes House is part of a continuum with transitional housing, job training, and Café Reyes, a space where men rebuild their lives with dignity.

In 2015, I was approached about becoming Commissioner of Health and Human Services for Worcester. I didn't even know what a commissioner did. But I applied, interviewed, and was hired.

Since then, we've led bold, unapologetic public health work.

We brought syringe exchange to Worcester. We fought stigma through education and advocacy. We launched the Housing First Council and Reentry Task Force. We helped bring suboxone into the jail system, understanding that recovery doesn't wait for release.

We created the HUB, a cross-agency collaboration supporting high-risk individuals. We started the Women Against Sexual Exploitation group, and from that came Jana's Place, a first-of-its-kind treatment home for trafficked women.

We stood up for comprehensive sex education. We confronted loneliness, mental health stigma, and inequity.

We launched the COVID Equity Task Force, which continues today, driving local action through data.

And in more recent years, we have pushed boundaries further: championing Overdose Prevention Centers, using opioid settlement funds to open a Black men's treatment center and housing for older adults, helping to bring permanent supportive housing to Worcester, including tiny homes for seniors built by volunteers.

Each of these programs was born from listening. Each step forward was rooted in compassion, evidence, and the belief that we can do better, and that we must.

This work was never about policy for the sake of policy. It was about people.

About believing in the dignity of every human being, housed or unhoused, free or incarcerated, well or struggling.

And it was always personal.

Because I never forgot that little girl in the glass box. Her tears. Her courage. Her belief that something better was possible.

That little girl now stands here, not just as a physician or a public servant, but as proof of what's possible when we invest in people. When we lead with heart. When we never stop believing in justice.

This foreword is not an ending—it is a threshold—a reminder that our stories are not just memories; they are maps.

In this book, Poderosa Latinas from diverse industries come together—leaders, visionaries, and changemakers—to share their truths, lift one another, and pave the way for those yet to come.

May their voices guide you to action, inspire hope, and ignite the audacity to believe that change is not only possible—it's already unfolding.

With deep gratitude,

Dr. Mattie Castiel
Commissioner of Health and Human Services, Worcester

Dr. Matilde Castiel is a Cuban-born physician and public health leader who served as Worcester's Commissioner of Health and Human Services from 2015 until her retirement in 2025. A compassionate advocate for equity and inclusion, she founded the Latin American Health Alliance (LAHA) to combat homelessness and addiction and continues to serve as its Medical Director. Dr. Castiel was on the founding Executive Committee of the Massachusetts Large Cities Health Collaborative and currently serves as its President.

Through her leadership at the city, state, and community levels, Dr. Castiel has dedicated her life to healing, empowering, and uplifting those most in need—a true ELLA Poderosa whose journey embodies courage, compassion, and service.

Introduction

WHY THIS BOOK EXISTS

This book was born out of legacy, love, and the quiet yet unshakable power of storytelling. For me, it began at the kitchen table, watching my mami embody generosity and resilience, and learning early on that *querer es poder*—where there is a will, there is a way. But more than that, I learned that no matter what doors life opens for us, the true measure of leadership is whether we hold that door open for others.

That is the heartbeat of this anthology.

Latinas have always been powerful, resourceful, and resilient. We carry generations of wisdom and sacrifice in our bones. We are daughters, mothers, sisters, professionals, business owners, leaders, and dreamers. Yet too often, our stories remain hidden— told only in kitchens, whispered at family tables, or buried under the weight of survival. Too often, we rise in silence, without recognition, without reflection, and without the space to honor the journey.

This anthology is our space. A safe place. A declaration that our voices matter, our stories matter, and our leadership matters. It is a reminder to every Latina—whether she is a student, a mother, an entrepreneur, or a community leader—that she is not alone in the challenges she faces, even as we celebrate the progress we have made.

THE WHY OF THIS BOOK

So why this book, and why now?

Because Latinas are still underrepresented in leadership across nearly every sector—business, politics, education, technology, healthcare, and beyond. We are nearly **20% of the U.S. population,** yet hold **less than 2% of executive leadership roles.** Latina entrepreneurs are starting businesses at **six times the national average,** but receive **less than 2% of venture capital funding.** And despite our growing presence, Latinas continue to face the **widest pay gap in America—earning just 52 cents for every dollar earned by white men.**

In STEM, the gap is even wider. Latinas make up just **2% of STEM jobs** and less than **10% of engineering roles,** despite entering these fields at growing rates. The barriers are not about talent, but about access, visibility, and belief. Too many Latinas have stayed away from STEM—not because they couldn't do the work, but because they had no role models who looked like them, and because of the persistent notion that you had to be "brilliant in math" to belong.

I know this firsthand. When I studied computer science in college, I was the only Latina and the only woman in my classes. I had no mentor who looked like me, no example of a Latina thriving in that field. In hindsight, the pressure to prove that I was more than capable pushed me harder—I ended up graduating with honors.

Even then, the proving didn't stop. As an IT consultant, I often had to show clients that I was not only capable, but worth the money I charged—because I refused to settle for 52 cents on the dollar, or less. And once I showed them what I could deliver, the contracts kept coming, and so did the money.

That experience stayed with me, and it shaped my mission. Part of the reason I created Empowering Latina Leaders Affirmation (ELLA) was to change that mindset and narrative. I wanted Latinas to have a safe place where they could see themselves reflected in leadership, where they would know they are not alone, and where mentoring and support are always within reach. Most of all, I wanted to build a space where Latinas no longer feel they must ask permission or prove their worth to belong—because they already do.

This book is here to make that rise visible. It is here to honor the Poderosa who lead in silence and those who lead with bold voices. It is here to remind us that leadership comes in many forms—sometimes with titles, often without them. It is here to capture the richness of our *Latinidad* and the strength we draw from it.

Most importantly, this book exists to leave a legacy for the next generation. Our daughters, our nieces, our students, and the young women watching us need to see themselves reflected in leadership and in literature. They need to know that their voices are not just welcome—they are needed.

WHAT THIS BOOK IS (AND IS NOT)

This anthology is a collection of real, raw, and powerful stories from Latinas who have lived them. Some are stories of resilience born in hardship. Others are stories of triumph, legacy, and leadership. Some are deeply personal, others professional. All are honest.

This book is not just a celebration of success—it is a testimony of the road it takes to get there. The vulnerability, the setbacks, the doubts, the sacrifices. The truth that leadership is not always glamorous, but it is always meaningful.

MY ROLE AS MAIN AUTHOR

As the main author, I carry two roles: storyteller and bridge-builder. My story is here because it is part of the foundation. But my greater mission has been to create a platform where other voices could rise too.

Through my work as President of the Latin American Business Organization (LABO) and Founder and President of Empowering Latina Leaders Affirmation (ELLA), I have seen firsthand the need for representation, for safe spaces, for mentorship, and for stories that tell the full truth of our journeys. This anthology is an extension of that mission.

ABOUT THE CONTRIBUTORS

The co-authors in these pages are *Poderosas.* They are leaders, entrepreneurs, advocates, professionals, educators, creatives, and visionaries. Some are well-known in their fields; others are the hidden leaders who make quiet yet powerful impact behind the scenes. They came from Central, South Central and Western Massachusetts, North Shore and beyond. They represent multiple generations, experiences, and perspectives.

Each woman has taken the courageous step to put her story into words—to be vulnerable, to be authentic, and to leave the door open for others to learn and rise.

THEMES YOU WILL FIND

As you read, you will find themes that bind these stories together:

- **Resilience** in the face of loss, struggle, or systemic barriers.
- **Imposter syndrome** and how we've learned to silence the voice that tells us we're not enough.
- **Cultural wealth**—embracing the gifts of our Latinidad as strengths, not obstacles.
- **Leadership without titles,** where Latinas lead with action, love, and vision rather than position.
- **Poderosa connections,** where Latinas mentor, support, uplift, and rise collectively with purpose.
- **Leaving the door open,** ensuring that each rise is not solitary, but collective.

THE READER'S PLACE

This book is for you, *querida lectora.*

If you are a Latina, may you see yourself in these pages. May you find strength, inspiration, and the reminder that you are Poderosa. May you know that your story matters.

If you are an ally, a colleague, or a leader outside our community, may these pages open your eyes and heart to the richness of Latina leadership and the barriers that still exist. May you join us in amplifying these voices.

CLOSING

This anthology is more than stories. It is a legacy. It is the power of Poderosas rising together.

It is the quiet but undeniable roar of Poderosas saying: *We are here, siempre hemos estado aquí, and we will continue to rise.*

Every story in these pages carries love, resilience, and faith. Every story is a door held open.

As you read, I invite you to reflect on your own story—on the doors that were opened for you, and on the doors you now hold open for others. Because leadership is not about walking through alone—it's about making sure others can walk through, too.

This book is my offering, my dedication, and my gratitude. To the women whose stories fill these pages. To my *mami, mi Reina sin Corona,* whose quiet strength shaped my purpose. And to you, dear reader, for stepping into this circle of voices.

May these pages inspire you to rise, to speak, and to lead with compassion, humility, and courage—always rooted in gratitude.

Because when one of us rises, we all rise. And great leaders never close the door behind them.

When Latinas join together, not only will we become an unbeatable force, but also a force for good.

And this is only the beginning. There will be more volumes, more stories, and more voices—because our legacy deserves to be written, shared, and remembered for generations to come.

THE JOURNEY OF A REINA SIN CORONA

ELIZABETH CRUZ

"Great Leaders Don't Close the Door Behind Them."

As Latinas, our nurturing spirit is part of our DNA. No matter how much we argue at the kitchen table—or how often we get upset over something as small as not receiving an official invitation from *nuestra tía o hermana* for *Noche Buena,* even though we've been going to their house every year—we still show up. We want the invitation not because we doubt that we're welcome, but because it's our way of feeling seen, included, respected, and valued.

That's the beauty and complexity of our culture. Family matters. We take care of each other, even through disagreements, distance, and generations.

My own story begins with that same spirit of family and openness. My mother Gloria Reyes Perez was the first in her family to relocate from Puerto Rico to Southbridge, Massachusetts, in the 1960s—a small town about 60 miles from Boston. She was a pioneer in her own quiet way, leaving everything familiar behind to build a life in a place where few spoke our language or looked like us.

I was the youngest of nine children, though one of my brothers drowned when I was just four years old. That loss marked our family deeply. Yet, even in the face of such heartbreak, my mother carried herself with faith and quiet resilience. She kept us together, reminding us through her actions that love, unity, and strength could carry us through anything.

Even though she carried the quiet regret of not insisting my brother come with her when she relocated to Southbridge, she transformed that pain into purpose. Determined to create a better life for her children, she built a new beginning from the ground up. But she didn't keep it to herself. One by one, her siblings, cousins, nieces, and nephews followed, staying in our crowded, lively apartment until they found a place of their own. My mother didn't hesitate. She kept the door open, always.

Looking back now, I realize that long before I ever said the words and created this quote, my mother lived them: "Great leaders don't close the door behind them."

In our household, *comida, bendición,* and *familia* were sacred. Every day began with a blessing and ended with a shared meal, no matter how busy or tired we were. The kitchen wasn't just where meals were cooked—it was where stories were told, advice was given, disagreements were resolved, and bonds were strengthened. Even when space was tight or money was short, my mother made sure there was always a plate to eat and a place to rest.

That upbringing shaped me. I learned what it meant to be selfless, to serve, and to show up for others—not because you expected anything in return, but because it was the right thing to do. I saw firsthand how one woman's courage could change the trajectory of an entire family.

We lived a modest, middle-class life. My mother worked until she became disabled, then devoted herself fully to home. My stepfather—the only father I've ever known—spoiled me with whatever I wanted, from the latest fashion to expensive 8-track tapes. My mother often shook her head, calling him crazy for spending money on such things.

I learned early on that *querer es poder*—where there is a will, there is a way. My stepfather never had the chance to attend school; instead, he worked alongside his father on the farm and later faced circumstances that kept him from learning to read or write. Yet through perseverance, he earned a decent living doing piecework in a factory.

Starting at just eight years old, I would sit with my stepfather at the kitchen table every night. The kitchen was big, with a breakfast table in the middle, always carrying the faint smell of *café con leche, comida frita* or *arroz con gandules*. His hands, rough from factory work and previous farm work, would wrap clumsily around the pen. At first, his strokes were shaky, the letters uneven, his frustration visible in the furrow of his brow. But each night, we tried again. I remember the moment his name first flowed across the page with steadiness—his smile lit up the room. He held the paper proudly, not just as proof of his signature, but as proof of his dignity. He could now sign his name with confidence and pride.

That simple ritual became a lesson in love, dignity, and the quiet strength that shaped my understanding of resilience.

My mother never had much of her own, yet whatever she did have—whether money, food, or comfort—she gave freely, without hesitation. Even when I was older and working as a software engineer consultant with a good salary, she was still giving. If she received a little extra—a refund, a gift, or a small lottery win—she quietly set some aside for me. And even though I was financially stable, I could never turn it down. Because I knew she wasn't just giving me money—she was giving me love.

When she and my stepfather separated during my high school years, she barely made ends meet. And yet, she lived with an abundance mindset—abundant love, abundant faith, and an open-door spirit. Even when it was just the two of us, she cooked a big meal every day, just in case someone stopped by. In her heart, there was always room for one more. She didn't lead with speeches or lessons. She led by example.

When I moved to Worcester for college, my mami didn't want to be alone. She begged me not to go—she would've preferred I got married and settled down instead. In fact, a successful Italian car dealer and my mother's social worker both wanted to pedir mi mano—but marriage wasn't even on my list! One was 10 years older, the other 22. I told her I wanted to travel the world and become a flight attendant. After a pause, she said, "Fine, I'll give you all my furniture," and decided to move in with one of my sisters. Giving me the furniture made her feel like she was contributing, like she was still supporting me. That was my mami—giving, expecting nothing in return. To this day, I still feel a little guilty for accepting it. But I've come to realize—that's what made her happy. Giving was her love language.

Looking back, I know that everything I am today—everything I've built, and the doors I now hold open for others—was modeled for me by a *Poderosa mujer (mi mami)* who gave everything she had. She never chased wealth, though she could have. She could have gone after my biological father's fortune or saved her money instead of giving it away. But she chose a different kind of richness—the kind that comes from love, sacrifice, and a legacy of service.

Even in her final breath, my mami was still giving. She offered advice to each of her loved ones who stood by her side—except me. I was there, holding her hand, watching her pour out final words of wisdom, but she said nothing to me. That silence broke me. Inside, I was falling apart.

I prayed, begging mi Diosito for just one moment alone with her before He took her away. And He answered.

When we were finally alone, I leaned in and asked gently, "Why didn't you give me advice, mami?"

She looked at me with her beaming hazel eyes—full of love, sadness, and deep gratitude. Her voice was soft but clear, "Ay, mija... I didn't want anyone in the room to feel jealous. Everyone already knows how proud I am of you—and you have it all. You didn't need advice—you're already walking in your purpose. And you know how I feel about you. You were always there for me— even doing the impossible, like finding that photo of mi Virgen del Socorro. Always making sure I was comfortable. Always protecting me. You know how much I love you."

In that sacred moment, I understood what she meant by "you have it all." It wasn't about money, perfection, or recognition. To her, I had it all because I knew who I was and where I was going. I had a career I loved, a family who loved me, a husband and son by my side, and a life rooted in service, faith, and gratitude. I was living the purposeful life she prayed for me—a life that lifted others.

That was her final gift. She saw me. She believed in me. And in her own quiet, powerful way, she reminded me that I was already living the lessons she had spent a lifetime showing me— not with speeches, but with example.

That sacred moment lives within me. It reminds me daily that my mami is still here—watching from heaven, guiding my steps, whispering wisdom in the stillness. Her love didn't end—it transformed. Her legacy didn't stop—it continues to shape everything I do. Whether I'm mentoring a young Latina entrepreneur, leading a community initiative, or facing a difficult decision, I feel her presence.

Her wisdom lives on—not just in memory, but in motion. In the way I advocate, build, serve, and show up. I am who I am because she showed me how to lead without a crown, how to love without limits, and how to always leave the door open for others to rise. Rooted in the values she lived—faith, humility, service, unity, and above all, gratitude—I carry her legacy into every room I enter, every conversation I have, and every life I touch.

I lead as the President of the Latin American Business Organization (LABO), a full business development center providing pathways for entrepreneurs—especially those from underrepresented communities—to rise, learn, and thrive. I am also the Founder and President of Empowering Latina Leaders Affirmation (ELLA), created to provide a safe place for Latinas—not only to see themselves reflected in leadership, but to know they are not alone, that mentoring and support are always within reach, even as we continue to face challenges in spite of all the progress we have made. My mission is to change that reality and reshape the narrative for the next generation of Latinas. Through summits, panels, workshops, and celebrations, we remind women that their voices, their stories, and their presence truly matter.

Today, when I stand before a room full of entrepreneurs,

students, or community leaders, I often hear my mother's voice echoing in my heart. "Leave the door open." It's not just a quote—it's my compass. I've seen women of all ages walk into ELLA events shy and uncertain, only to leave standing taller, their voices stronger—forming bonds and new connections, supporting and uplifting each other, learning from one another, and walking away empowered, inspired, and appreciated as we honor and recognize their leadership and impact, with a renewed sense of being Poderosa, embracing their Latinidad, and moving forward more intentional than ever. But more importantly, I always ask: **Who are you bringing forward with you as you rise; opening doors and creating space for others to do the same?**

I've watched youth, men, and women walk into LABO with nothing but a bag of dreams and an idea—sometimes confused about their next steps, burdened with IRS issues, or even on the verge of losing their business—and then walk out standing taller, with a business plan, an action plan, a certification to move them forward, or simply the courage to take the next step. Each time, I recognize the look in their eyes—it's the same look I once saw in my stepfather's face at the kitchen table when he signed his name with pride. That moment taught me something eternal; leadership isn't about what you achieve for yourself, but how you empower others to rise. That is the legacy I inherited—and the one I now live to pass on.

I am an entrepreneur, investor, and real estate strategist, helping families build generational wealth and make empowered decisions—because mi señora taught me that having a home isn't just about ownership, it's about stability, dignity, and legacy. I've helped over 600 families find their space, and in doing so, I've found mine.

I advocate across platforms—from local and global chambers to state-wide events, from the Worcester WooSox Wepa Games to business expos—because representation doesn't happen by chance. It happens by showing up. And I don't just show up for myself—I show up for us. For the single mother. For the girl who's told she's too loud or too much. For the family starting over. For the Latina who doesn't yet know she's a leader.

My mission is not to be known or popular—it is to make an impact. To unite people. To amplify stories. To push for systems that reflect our worth. Because when our community wins, everyone wins.

My mami didn't just raise me. She raised a leader. A bridge-builder. A problem solver. A voice for those still waiting for their turn. And while I never asked for titles, I carry many with pride—mother, wife, mentor, friend, advocate, coach, entrepreneur, storyteller, songwriter, *Poderosa,* and *Líder.* Along the way, the community gave me others: *la alcaldesa de Worcester* and now, *Reina sin Corona.* Each name reflects the lives I've touched and the love I've poured into my purpose.

If I could leave one piece of advice, it would be this: Don't wait for permission to lead. Don't shrink to fit in. Know who you are, walk in your purpose, and when you rise—hold the door open. Someone is always waiting for your light to shine on their path.

And if I had to be remembered by just one sentence, it would be this: She rose, but never alone.

She held the door open and changed everything.

ADVICE THAT CHANGED MY LIFE

The advice that changed my life came from my oldest sister. She once told me, *"You can't change people or be responsible for their actions."* At the time, I didn't realize how powerful those words would become. I've always been the one to step in, to help, to fix, to carry others through their struggles. But her words taught me the difference between guiding someone and trying to live their journey for them.

That advice gave me peace and strength. It reminded me that leadership isn't about control—it's about influence, example, and faith. Faith in yourself, in others, and in the process of becoming. We can open doors, but others must choose to walk through them. Later, my mentor added a deeper truth: while it's important to leave the door open for others, it's just as important to protect your own purpose. Be mindful not to let anyone anchor you down or drain your energy. Not everyone is meant to have a seat at your table, and that's okay.

I've learned that boundaries may challenge others, but they're essential to staying grounded in your purpose and peace.

Keep the door open, bring someone forward, but never at the cost of your own peace or purpose.

Biography

Elizabeth Cruz is the Founder and President of Empowering Latina Leaders Affirmation (ELLA) and the President of the Latin American Business Organization (LABO). She also serves as a steering committee member of *Unidos in Power*, amplifying her advocacy for representation, equity, and community empowerment. Through LABO, she leads a full business development center that supports entrepreneurs of all backgrounds—men and women alike—helping them start, grow, and sustain their businesses with education, certification, and advocacy.

With a degree in computer science and more than 20 years of experience in information technology, consulting, and real estate, Elizabeth blends technical expertise with business strategy and a steadfast commitment to empowerment. Her journey—from being the only Latina and woman in her computer science classes to becoming an IT consultant, real estate strategist, and community leader—shaped her mission to open doors for others and change the narrative of what leadership looks like for Latinas. She is guided by her quote: *Great leaders don't close the door behind them.*

Elizabeth is also a creative voice, writing poetry, songs, and stories that reflect resilience, faith, and cultural pride. She is a contributing author in Hispanic Star Rising Volume IV, further amplifying her voice and commitment to storytelling as a tool for empowerment.

Through ELLA, she has created a safe space where Latinas can see themselves reflected in leadership, mentor one another, and rise collectively. Beyond her visionary leadership, she has helped over 600 families build generational wealth through real estate.

A proud wife, mother, and storyteller, songwriter, Elizabeth carries her mother's legacy of love, resilience, and gratitude into every room, every conversation, and every life she touches.

Elizabeth Cruz has been widely recognized for her leadership, community impact, and professional excellence. In 2024, she was honored with the **ALX100 Award,** the **United Way Women's Initiative Lois B. Green Leadership Award,** and named among **Worcester Business Journal's Power 100.** Previously, she was also celebrated as one of the **Outstanding Women in Business** (2022). In real estate, Elizabeth's commitment to excellence earned her recognition from **Keller Williams Realty as a Million Dollar Club member (2019)** and ranked **#3 in Sold Listing Volume and #5 in Closed Sales Volume (2020).**

Elizabeth Cruz

liz.reinasincorona@gmail.com

https://www.linkedin.com/in/ecdejesus/

https://www.instagram.com/liz_reinasincorona/

A NEW BEGINNING IN A NEW LAND

ADRIANA SIEMASZKO

"The most important thing we can leave our children isn't just financial support. It's a legacy of inner growth, spiritual strength, and strong principles that help them face life with purpose and direction."

DEDICATION

To my beloved husband, Richad, and my son, David Stiven. you are my strength in difficult moments and my peace within our home.

Your unconditional love has given me the courage to move forward and the refuge to keep fighting not only for my dreams, but to help create a path for those who will come after me and for our family. David, son you are my hero love you.

In my work as a community leader, I see myself as the pawn in a game of chess. Quiet, humble, and guided by the belief that my purpose is to serve others. Every step I take is meant to support the greater good and give back to the Latino community and to my family for everything life has given me.

Each day, I focus on building connections between people and the opportunities that exist, often hidden behind language barriers or a lack of information. I lead programs that empower our community to find resources, pursue a more dignified life, and secure that first job which, for many, marks the beginning of a new chapter in this country. I work hand-in-hand with local and government organizations that offer valuable tools, although these are often out of reach for those who need them most.

I believe that true impact is made through consistent commitment. Every action I take is an act of faith. It means facing the fears and challenges that come with being an immigrant. Today, I am surrounded by strong leaders and people who carry the knowledge and resources our community needs. Even so, I always keep my team in mind, our partners, and every person who, from a quiet corner, is still hoping for a better opportunity.

CHALLENGES

Before coming to the United States, I built a strong career in Colombia. I worked for respected companies in the healthcare field and held key roles as a medical representative. But everything changed when I immigrated at 45, not speaking English and stepping into an entirely unfamiliar world.

Like many immigrant professionals, I had to start from the beginning. I quickly realized how hard it was to find resources or information in Spanish. What I expected to be available simply wasn't. That's when I decided to create Latinos Buscando Trabajo, my first social media page dedicated to sharing job opportunities with our community. With the help of my son, David Echavarria, who was still in high school at the time, we began the mission of making essential information available in both English and Spanish for people like me, people simply searching for a chance

I studied English for eight months at Clark University. My goal was to keep learning, but then came the opportunity of a lifetime: an interview at Masis Staffing. At the time, my English was at an upper-intermediate level. One of the owners, Frankie Vaccaro, along with the manager of that office, saw potential in me because of my work experience and personal story. However, not everyone agreed. Another executive on the team had a different opinion, and in the end, they chose someone else for the position.

One month later, I received an unexpected call. A woman from Masis told me that the person they had hired was in an accident on their first day and would be out for several weeks. They offered me the position, and my office would be in Webster, MA.

From day one, the team welcomed me with warmth. Most of the people coming in for jobs were Latino, and with my son's help, we created a strategy to post openings in Spanish. That's how it all began. And little by little, the magic of connecting with the community looking for opportunities and a job started to unfold.

We began forming partnerships with companies and organizations supported by the state. The first to open their doors to us was CENTRO in Worcester. With the same commitment to serve, we started organizing job fairs and sharing helpful information for the Puerto Rican and broader Latin American communities. Over time, we built a brand with its own identity and started gaining recognition. Our mission was no longer just for Latinos. The work we did began to support other communities as well.

We posted job openings and attended fairs and events on Saturdays, Sundays, and even late into the evenings. We didn't stop. Our commitment was full and consistent, because we knew there was always someone out there waiting for an opportunity. The work was demanding, but it had purpose. We made sure that in every corner, someone could find information and a reason to keep going.

I learned that no matter how humble your job may be, you should always give it your best. With the constant support of my son, David Echavarria, who came with me to every event, we were able to open doors in Boston, Worcester, Providence, and beyond. Together, we created 18 bilingual pages to share job opportunities and resources, not only from Masis Staffing but also from our partners. Our dedication helped build a brand that became respected for its impact on the community.

Everywhere I went, I saw an opportunity. One day, I went to the Colombian consulate to renew my passport. There, I met Consul Xida, the Colombian general consul at the time. I explained that I wanted to help newly arrived Colombians who didn't know where to begin their job search. Not only did she see me without an appointment, but she also shared our job listings on the embassy's website. Months later, I received an invitation to a meeting with ten consuls from different Latin American countries. That moment was the door God opened.

Since then, we've worked alongside the consulates of Mexico, Guatemala, El Salvador, Honduras, and others. For more than nine years, we have participated in job fairs, offered guidance, and joined mobile consulate events. To each of these diplomatic leaders, I extend my sincere gratitude.

Presenting our program to ambassadors and consuls was intimidating, but also an incredible experience. I felt proud to see how committed these high-ranking officials are to supporting their people. Every one of them opened their doors and helped share our information. Today, many of those consulates still count on us as partners in their community programs. Our goal remains the same: to serve with empathy, to build bridges, and to create opportunities for those who, like me, once came to this country looking for a fresh start.

AS AN INDIVIDUAL AND AS A COMMUNITY LEADER

On a personal level, my goal is inner growth, especially in times of uncertainty. You reach a point in life where you begin to question what lies beyond the constant struggle to stand out. We forget that every day is one less. Each change and each challenge has pushed me to find new ways forward and to recognize opportunities I hadn't noticed before.

This journey showed me how people adapt when they really need to. As long as they have a clear goal and the determination to grow without ever stepping over others. I realized that transitions are not obstacles, but starting points for developing ideas, creating new paths, and discovering chances that wouldn't have appeared otherwise.

Today, I'm grateful for every one of those experiences. They helped me expand my perspective and understand that real growth happens when we dare to step outside our comfort zone. Starting over gave me the chance to launch projects, build relationships, and find new possibilities, even in unfamiliar territory.

Throughout my career, I've come to understand that much of what I've achieved comes from making the most of every opportunity. From my earliest steps in my home country, whether out of financial need or an inner strength that has always guided me, I knew I wanted to excel in every task I took on, no matter how small it seemed.

When I arrived in this country, I learned that having a clear goal is important, but not enough. Behind every goal, there must be something even stronger: motivation. In my case, that motivation came from within. It was the force that pushed me forward, even in uncertain moments. A goal is something you aim to reach, while motivation is what gives you the energy to keep going.

I believe everyone needs to find a reason that gives their life meaning. It could be yourself, your family, your career, or a dream that lives deep in your heart. For me, that reason has always been my son, David. He became the source of my strength, the reason I pushed forward, the inspiration to lead by example. I wanted to shine without competing with anyone else, only with myself, and to prove that success is possible without losing your values. The most important thing we can leave our children isn't just financial support. It's a legacy of inner growth, spiritual strength, and strong principles that help them face life with purpose and direction.

THE VULNERABILITY OF BEING HUMAN WHEN SEARCHING FOR WORK

Over the years, life has shown me both the best and, at times, the most difficult sides of human nature. Those experiences helped keep me grounded and made me appreciate even more the chance that God or the universe, however you choose to see it, gave me to be in this position.

When someone is looking for work, especially as a Latino immigrant just starting the American Dream, not speaking the language, sometimes without stable housing or close family nearby, it's easy to become vulnerable and guarded. We start to feel judged, misunderstood, or simply left out. And it's true. Language barriers create gaps that can easily become our biggest obstacles. We begin to believe ideas that hold us back and make our dreams feel unreachable.

From where I stood, I was helping my community during a time when many were lost and unsure how to begin again in a new country. They were in a place of need. I was in a place of abundance, not because of money, but because I had something deeper to offer. I could guide them to housing, connect them with their community, help them find churches, doctors, legal aid, and a sense of belonging. And yes, employment too…but I came to see that a job on its own is not enough without access to the other things that make life whole.

That's how you become a complete resource for the community. And as you serve, you grow, not just professionally, but as a person. Watching how these opportunities completely changed people's lives has filled me with lasting gratitude. It's become a way of life: to always give. And the circle always finds its way back.

We have a responsibility to follow the rules, to be examples, and to contribute to the country that welcomed us. We didn't come to be a burden. We came to be part of the solution. Be a reflection of the best parts of our culture. Help others rise. Share what you know. That circle of gratitude will always return. That is where the real magic in life exists: in giving without expecting, in serving with heart, and in building bridges for those who come after us.

At the end of the day, it's simple. We receive what we give. And the biggest limits we face are the ones we believe are real.

Biography

Adriana Siemaszko is a Colombian mother, immigrant, and community leader with a passion for creating opportunity where it's needed most. After building a successful career in healthcare sales in Colombia, she moved to the United States at age 45, not knowing the language but determined to give her family a better future.

Faced with the challenges of starting over, she created Latinos Buscando Trabajo, a bilingual platform to connect immigrants to jobs and essential resources. With her son, David Echavarria, she began publishing opportunities in both English and Spanish, reaching those often left out of traditional systems.

She now leads a national program that works with consulates, nonprofits, and companies like Masis Staffing to support communities across the country. Her work focuses on resource accessibility and community education.

To her, a job is just the beginning. True transformation happens when people are given the tools to build a life with dignity and hope. "

Adriana Siemaszko

Adriana_4021@hotmail.com

https://www.linkedin.com/in/adriana-s-99a99545/

https://www.facebook.com/Trabajosenmassachusetts

CHOOSING TO BUILD MY LEGACY THROUGH SERVICE

ADRIANA VACCARO

"If you dare to dream big, the path will begin to form in front of you. The key is to take the first step, even when your knees are shaking. Even when people say you can't. Especially then."

DEDICATION

To my mother, María Zully Moreno, for teaching me that I can be whatever I decide to be. Your faith in me made everything possible.

This is a story about possibilities, opportunities, and, most importantly, legacy. I would like my words to be a personal invitation to heal, transform, and to create.

I was born in Bogota, Colombia, the youngest of three children. I had a happy upbringing. I remember Christmas with my mom, going to church, and having a normal life. I also remember being painfully aware of disparities between my siblings and me.

My older brother and sister had a father with wealth and status. Private security, limousines, brand-new cars for their birthdays. Meanwhile, my father, who had very little, passed away in a car accident when I was just six years old. That loss shaped me in more ways than I can count. While we were one family, I always felt some sort of misfit vibe.

I grew up with a front-row seat to disparity. Each Christmas Eve, I watched my siblings opening their presents. They were 22 and 23 at the time. I was just seven. And though I didn't fully understand why there was nothing under the tree for me, I watched with excitement and curiosity. I was happy for them. I didn't question it, until I got older.

That contrast lit a fire in me. I promised myself I would never be in the position my mother was, without options, without the ability to give her youngest daughter what she longed to. I became fiercely independent, determined to create a different future.

When I moved to the United States, I came with one goal:

to become solvent and generous. To create a life where no one around me had to feel the absence I once felt. I wanted to give to those left out, overlooked, or under-resourced.

Today, that's one of the greatest joys of my life. Not just the financial stability I've built, but what it allows me to give back—to others, to the work I care about, and especially to my mother. Now in her 70s, she gives to causes that matter to her, not because she has to, but because she can. She is no longer a woman limited by circumstance. She is part of a legacy of generosity that we're writing together.

Empowerment, for me, isn't about success alone. It's about healing generational lack, creating dignity where there was disparity, and building a legacy that says: We rise, and we give.

The greatest lesson I've learned came from a simple book written by Dr. Wayne Dyer that said: "Nobody owes you anything." That truth changed everything for me. It initiated my healing journey. My mother, my father, my family, nobody was responsible for my life other than me. I could hide behind excuses, or I could simply create a new reality. Life isn't about handouts or free passes, it's about giving, showing up, and doing the best we can with what we have from where we are.

So, to any Latina sisters reading this, dismantle your mental blocks. It doesn't matter if you're the first in your family. It doesn't matter where you live, how much education you have, or what you didn't have growing up. If you start pouring service into others, if you focus on legacy while you're still here, you will be amazed by the woman you become.

RECIPROCITY: THE INFINITE MULTIPLIER

Reciprocity isn't what I first imagined it to be. Growing up, I thought it was a simple exchange—you help someone, and, eventually, that person helps you. A tidy ledger of give and take. Maybe it's cultural, or maybe it's human nature, but I used to think that reciprocity worked like a balance sheet. But what I've come to understand through experience, disappointment, and unexpected blessings, is that real reciprocity is not transactional. It's not linear. And it's certainly not something you can track or tally. True reciprocity is an infinite game. It's a multiplier, not a calculator.

Here's what that means in real life: When you do something kind, generous, or helpful for someone, it's not your job to expect a return. Your role ends at the giving. The return, if it comes, may not come from the same person, or even the same direction. Sometimes it circles back in ways you couldn't have planned or predicted.

I've helped people who never even said thank you. And that's completely okay. Because I've also been on the receiving end of unimaginable generosity from people I never expected. Doors have opened, introductions have been made, and support has arrived from surprising places, not because I kept score, but because I kept giving.

The moment I stopped keeping track was the moment I stepped into abundance. Generosity isn't a strategy; it's a way of being. And when you live that way, reciprocity becomes something greater than a favor returned. It becomes a current that carries you forward, connecting you to people, opportunities, and blessings you never saw coming.

DON'T LET ANYONE DEFINE YOUR LIMITS

Don't let anyone tell you what you should or shouldn't do. Not the internet. Not your family. Not your spouse. And definitely not that quiet but persistent voice in your head that tries to protect you by keeping you small.

I'll never forget the day I sat across from someone I admired, a person I thought could help me step into a new opportunity. I told him I was thinking about investing in a three-decker property. His face tightened. Then came the words that landed like a punch to the gut: "You're a single mom with a full-time job. You can't be serious about buying a three-decker." He followed it up with something even more condescending, "Why don't you just relax? Maybe take a yoga class. Real estate isn't for people like you."

That moment shook me. For a split second, I believed him. I felt embarrassed. Like I had just reached too far above my station. Like I needed to shrink back into the version of myself that felt safe and predictable.

But thank God I didn't stay there.

Instead of letting his doubts become my limits, I turned them into fuel. I got quiet. I made a plan. I did the work. And that three-decker? I bought it. That dream? It became my reality.

Here's what I know for sure: If you dare to dream big, the path *will* begin to form in front of you. The key is to take the first step, even when your knees are shaking. Even when people say you can't. Especially then.

Never let someone else's limited vision block your unlimited potential. The world needs your courage. Your ambition. Your "crazy" ideas. So, tune out the noise and bet on yourself. There is no substitute for doing something you *absolutely love*. That one thing that lights you up, keeps you curious, and pulls you forward, even on hard days. That's the thing that makes you unstoppable.

For me, that thing is organizational culture. My obsession with human behavior and how we treat one another has been part of my life for as long as I can remember. As a child, I didn't have the language for it, but I was always observing, always studying how people made others feel, how they built (or broke) trust, and how the energy in a room could shift with just one word or one action.

Now, years later, that curiosity is the foundation of my business. Culture work is humanistic work. It's not just about policies and mission statements. It's about how we act, react, and interact. It's about the tone we set in our workplaces, our families, and our communities. And after 17 years, I'm still excited to do the work every single day. I help organizations and their leaders build cultures where people thrive. Through a blend of leadership development, employee coaching, people analytics, and organizational culture consulting, I equip teams to align values, improve engagement, and drive performance. My work is about creating workplaces that inspire trust, collaboration, and growth, so businesses succeed while people feel fulfilled."

I feel incredibly lucky to have found something that makes me want to get better, keep learning, and show up with purpose. Every session, every client, every challenge brings me energy. And yes, building a financial legacy is important. But the greatest gift I want to give my three sons is not a portfolio. It's an example. I want them to see their mother waking up with intention, doing work that matters, and living a life fueled by passion and gratitude. I want them to know that it's possible to build a career not just for survival, but for joy. That loving what you do isn't a fantasy, it's a standard worth pursuing.

So, on that note, find your thing. The one that makes you feel unstoppable. And when you do, pour your whole self into it. That's how you create a legacy that lives far beyond the work.

If there's one truth that echoes through every part of my journey, it's this: We're not meant to do life, or leadership, alone. Every moment of growth in my path has been sparked by connection, fueled by service, and anchored in purpose. Whether it was refusing to listen to limiting beliefs, embracing the long game of reciprocity, or choosing to build a life around what I love; I've learned that impact doesn't happen in isolation. It happens when we show up for others. When we pour into community. When we lead with both courage and heart.

So, as you turn the page on this chapter, I want to leave

you with this call: Connect with others not because you need something, but because you have something to give. Serve not out of obligation, but because generosity is a form of leadership. And build your legacy not by chasing applause, but by creating meaning.

We rise higher when we rise together. If anything I've shared has inspired you, challenged you, or reminded you of your own power, I invite you to reach out. Let's keep the conversation going. Let's build, dream, and lead lives that matter.

Because the world needs more Latinas Poderosas who are lit up by their purpose, and unafraid to pass that light on.

ADVICE THAT CHANGED MY LIFE

Calladita no more! Keeping your head down and letting your work do the talk is an outdated and ineffective strategy. Be proud of your identify, be bold about your mission. That was advice from one of my coaches, Sara Connell. She always preaches: "be for something" meaning, have a reason, a goal, a value that guides you. And also "be against nothing." If you don't like what someone is doing simply don't engage. Do not spend your beautiful and powerful energy on fighting someone else's vision. Use every ounce of energy you have on missions that align with yours. Collectively we are a force so let's not dilute our power.

Biography

Adriana Vaccaro is an award-winning entrepreneur, organizational culture strategist, and best-selling author dedicated to transforming the way we work by centering people, purpose, and performance. Originally from Bogota, Colombia, Adriana's journey is one of resilience, vision, and relentless commitment to building workplaces where humanity and strategy coexist.

With a career in human resources and process improvement, Adriana has spent over 15 years helping organizations align their people practices with their business goals. Her work bridges behavioral science, data, and culture change, guiding leaders through complex transformations that elevate trust, collaboration, and inclusion.

She is the founder and CEO of Culture Redesigned, a consulting firm that partners with mission-driven organizations to build cultures of belonging and innovation. Under her leadership, the firm has delivered measurable results for clients across sectors, empowering executive teams, improving employee engagement, and increasing organizational effectiveness through data-informed culture strategies.

Adriana is also the author of *Culture-Minded: Six Tools to Transform Organizational Culture and Empower Humanity*, an Amazon best-seller that blends research, practical tools, and real-world case studies.

A passionate advocate for equity, inclusion, and continuous improvement, Adriana is often invited to speak on leadership, organizational transformation, and the power of human-centered design in the workplace. She is known for her ability to connect across cultures, inspire reflection, and catalyze meaningful change. She was born in Colombia and currently lives in Massachusetts with her husband and three sons.

Adriana Vaccaro

adriana@cultureredesigned.com

https://www.linkedin.com/in/adrianavaccaro/

https://www.cultureredesigned.com/

FINDING MY RHYTHM: AN AUTHENTIC
JOURNEY INTO LEADERSHIP

ANABELLE SANTIAGO

"Your playing small does not serve the world."
- Marianne Williamson

DEDICATION

This chapter is dedicated to my parents: to my mother, one of the strongest women I know, whose resilience has shaped me, and to my father, whose unwavering support has made every dream feel possible. Thank you to Claudia Paiva, Leah Larson, and Elizabeth Cruz for your mentorship, for guiding and uplifting me, for believing in my potential before I believed in it myself, and for modeling the kind of leadership I strive to embody.

Traditional images of leadership often depict someone bold, fearless, and commanding, a person whose confidence fills the room, whose words carry weight, and whose decisions seem unshakable. From an early age, I absorbed the idea that leadership came not just with presence, but with age, experience, and a certain authority that seemed unattainable without years of trial and perseverance. To be a leader, I assumed, you had to have walked more years, faced more challenges, and accumulated wisdom that only time could grant.

For someone like me, naturally quiet, reflective, and cautious, these assumptions were intimidating. Leadership seemed like an exclusive club, reserved for those who could command attention without hesitation. I watched others step into rooms with certainty, their presence undeniable, their decisions unshakable. I admired them deeply. And yet, despite my desire to belong, I felt distant, as if peering through a glass wall, too small and too soft-spoken to step through.

When I look at myself now, I still see the girl I once was, standing in the corner of a dance studio, quiet and observant, listening closely to the beat before daring to take the first step. She knew the rhythm and felt it deeply, but she was not sure she was meant to take center stage. That girl carried a persistent tension, a quiet knowing that she wanted more, even if she did not yet trust herself to reach for it. She held a world of potential tightly contained, waiting for permission that would never come from anyone but herself.

This is not a story of conquering endless obstacles or achieving perfection. It is a story of what happens when you begin to silence the inner critic, when you stop waiting for permission, and when you start leading in your own rhythm.

Dance became my first tangible way of exploring what I now recognize as my poderosa spirit. My mother enrolled me in classes at a young age, hoping to coax me out of my shell. I was shy and introverted, the kind of child teachers called "mature for her age," though that simply meant I stayed quiet and followed every rule. My parents, first-generation Dominican immigrants, carried dreams far beyond the circumstances they inherited. My father worked multiple jobs to provide for us, and my mother's love was expressed through opportunity, signing me up for sports, classes, and every activity that might help me find my voice. Yet, none of it fit quite right until I found dance.

At first, it was ballet, jazz, and tap—structured, precise, and disciplined, much like the child I was. I found joy in mastering steps and keeping pace with rhythm, but I still held back, cautious not to draw too much attention. In my preteen years, I discovered Latin dance, and everything shifted. The music felt like home. Its rhythm resonated in my body, and the movements carried a freedom and energy that demanded more than technical perfection. They required presence, courage, and self-expression. This was more than a change in dance style. It mirrored a pivotal time in my adolescence. As I navigated peer pressures and the search for identity, Latin dance drew me closer to my culture and heritage, inviting me to step into a space that had always felt slightly out of reach.

Even then, confidence did not come naturally. I danced cautiously, afraid to misstep or stand out too much. Over time, I realized that dance, like leadership, is not about flawless execution. It is about presence. It is about trusting yourself enough to take the next step, even when the choreography is uncertain, even when the rhythm feels intimidating.

Dance taught me more than self-expression. It taught me courage and self-trust. It showed me that leadership does not have to be loud, commanding, or performative to be meaningful. It can be deliberate, authentic, and deeply grounded in your own values, the same qualities that would later guide me as I began to navigate leadership in other spaces.

While dance helped me discover confidence, life outside the studio demanded another kind of leadership, one rooted in care, consistency, and responsibility. Around that same time, my family began serving as a foster home for children in transition. Our household became a revolving door of stories, heartbreaks, and second chances. I learned early what it meant to care for others, to listen, to comfort, and to create safety in spaces that did not always feel safe. Caregiving became second nature. It was how I expressed love, how I found purpose, and how I realized that leadership is relational and grounded in service, not status or authority.

That sense of purpose carried me through high school

and into the uncertainty of college, a journey that began amid the global pandemic. The world felt paused, uncertain, and overwhelming, yet I carried with me a quiet drive to be of service. My first professional experience was with the Latino Education Institute in partnership with my local Department of Public Health, where I served as a trusted messenger to communities that were often underrepresented. I helped bridge gaps in information, connect families to critical resources, and provide guidance where access had been limited. The work was meaningful, necessary, and at times daunting, but it opened my eyes to the power of advocacy and the responsibility that comes with it.

In that role, I met my first mentor, a woman whose belief in me and commitment to my growth became a guiding light. She not only encouraged me to step into new responsibilities, but she also took me along to network with her, introducing me to leaders and decision-makers in public health and philanthropy—people I might never have encountered on my own. She showed me how authentic leadership looks in action: compassionate, deliberate, and rooted in service. Through her, I learned that leadership is not only about authority or accolades but also about lifting others, creating opportunities, and showing up consistently. This mentorship planted the seed for my understanding of what it means to lead with both confidence and care.

Following that experience, I had the opportunity to support projects across Massachusetts focused on closing equity gaps in public health services. Each project deepened my understanding of systemic inequities and revealed who was often missing from the tables where decisions were made, especially women and girls. That awareness reignited a familiar spark, one I had first felt as a child watching my dance instructor lead with confidence and later as a college student watching my mentor open doors I never imagined I could enter. Those moments taught me that representation is not simply inspiring; it is transformational.

That same spark eventually led me to an internship with the United Way of Central Massachusetts Women's Initiative, a volunteer-driven women's philanthropy group dedicated to uniting voices and resources to uplift girls through programs designed just for them. What began as a requirement for class credit soon became a turning point in my journey. I found myself surrounded by a network of women leaders who not only led with confidence but also used their influence to create spaces where girls could explore their potential, build confidence, and thrive.

Within that network, I met another mentor, my supervisor, whose guidance continues to shape my path. She saw something in me before I fully saw it in myself. Her leadership and belief in my abilities opened new doors and helped me see that my own growth could inspire others. Witnessing her and so many other women lead with authenticity and generosity reinforced my understanding that leadership is not about control or recognition. It is about creating opportunity and making space for others to rise.

In time, that same mentor encouraged me to step into a leadership position, a promotion that would allow me to expand on the work I was already passionate about while taking on greater responsibility. It was an opportunity to deepen my impact and continue learning from women who had once guided me. The offer should have felt like a moment of triumph, yet it was layered with fear and uncertainty. I questioned whether I had enough experience, whether I could truly lead, or whether I would falter in the face of expectations. My inner critic whispered constantly: Do you belong here? Can you really do this? What if you fail?

More than anything, it felt like a leap in time, an opportunity I thought was still years away. I imagined that leadership roles like this came after a long stretch of experience and preparation. To be considered for one so soon felt both thrilling and intimidating, as though I had suddenly been fast-forwarded into a future version of myself I was still learning to grow into. But how could I turn down the chance to continue work that aligned so deeply with my purpose, work that empowered girls to silence their own doubts and step into their potential? The irony was not lost on me. I was stepping into a role that allowed me to be part of a movement supporting girls to lead with confidence, to trust themselves, and to pursue opportunities without letting their inner critic hold them back, the very lessons I was still learning myself.

So, I took the leap. I said yes, not because I felt entirely ready, but because someone believed in my potential and reminded me that growth rarely comes from certainty. If I waited for the perfect moment, I might never move at all. Leadership, like dance, begins in motion.

Since then, my leadership has become less about directing a performance and more about dancing in community. I come from a culture that believes in collective thriving, where success is measured not by individual achievement but by the ways we lift one another. To me, leadership is about creating spaces where others feel seen, valued, and safe to take their own leap of faith.

The mentorship I have received along the way did more than open doors. It taught me not to settle and to always believe I am capable of more. That lesson has transcended far beyond my career; it has shaped how I approach challenges, relationships, and personal growth. It taught me that abundance, love, and purpose flow when we trust ourselves to step forward, even when the choreography is still unfolding.

In these next chapters of my life, I am deeply committed to doing the same for other girls by giving back, opening doors, and leading by example. I want to help create spaces where girls feel empowered to take up space, speak up, and see themselves as leaders in their own right. My hope is to model that leadership is not about perfection or fearlessness. It is about showing up with authenticity, compassion, and courage, even when your voice shakes.

I am a young leader, still learning, still growing, and still stepping into spaces that challenge and stretch me. Some days, I feel as though I am catching up to the version of myself I am becoming, learning to inhabit this newfound confidence. Yet, with every moment of self-doubt, every stumble, and every small victory, I am reminded that leadership is not a destination; it is a dance. It is a rhythm of growth, grace, and resilience.

My goal is to lead by example, to navigate growth, setbacks, and uncertainty with honesty and humility, and to show that self-doubt is a normal part of the journey. What matters is that we keep moving forward despite it. By sharing my story and showing that leadership takes many forms, I hope to inspire young women to step boldly into spaces that may intimidate them and realize that the confidence and power to lead have always been within them.

ADVICE THAT CHANGED MY LIFE

The most impactful advice I've ever received was: *"You grow most in the spaces where you feel the most uncomfortable."* Comfort is easy and appealing - it feels safe and predictable, but if you envision more for yourself, you cannot settle. Progress and learning rarely happen in comfort. If you wait until everything feels safe and certain, you risk standing still, watching opportunities pass by while growth happens elsewhere. True development comes from stepping into uncertainty, embracing challenges, and testing your limits.

Leaning into discomfort allows you to discover strengths you didn't know you had. It teaches resilience, sharpens judgment, and builds self-trust. It also reminds you that failure isn't the opposite of success—it's part of the journey toward it.

My advice to readers is to approach every new opportunity with openness. Step forward even when doubt creeps in, take small risks, and allow yourself to make mistakes along the way. The moments that feel intimidating or uncertain are often the ones that shape your perspective, expand your capabilities, and reveal your true potential. Growth doesn't require perfection; it requires courage, curiosity, and the willingness to keep moving forward, even when it feels uncomfortable.

Biography

Anabelle Santiago is the Manager of the Women's Initiative at the United Way of Central Massachusetts, a women's philanthropy and volunteer network dedicated to reducing violence affecting adolescent girls through girls-only programming. She coordinates events, engages donors, and builds strategic partnerships, fostering a community of women creating safe, empowering spaces that help girls thrive and realize their potential.

A proud Latina and Summa Cum Laude graduate of Worcester State University in 2024, Anabelle holds a B.S. in public health and business administration with a minor in economics. She began advancing equity in community health, working with local health departments and the Latino Education Institute to address disparities in underserved neighborhoods, and served as a trusted messenger during the COVID-19 pandemic, supporting resource navigation and translation services.

Anabelle serves on the boards of ELLA (Empowering Latina Leaders Affirmation) and Ritmos Dance Company, leading initiatives of representation, empowerment, and opening doors for the next generation. She has been recognized with the 2024 Meridith D. Wesby Young Leader Award and the 2024 Greater Worcester Health Equity Award.

Beyond her work, she loves music and dance, is an avid traveler who has visited over 14 countries, enjoys exploring new foods and cultures, and cherishes time with loved ones.

Anabelle Santiago

anabelle.santiago@unitedwaycm.org

www.linkedin.com/in/anabelle-santiago

APUESTO A MÍ: A DAUGHTER'S LEGACY

DÉBORAH L. GONZÁLEZ, PH.D.

"I write to honor the women who came before me and the ones still rising, imperfectly but boldly, day by day and always betting on ourselves. Always saying, "Apuesto a mí."

DEDICATION

To my beloved daughters, Adria Westort and Sophia A. Westort González

Our path together has not always been smooth, yet through every twist and storm, love has been our compass. You are my inspiration, my pride, and the proof that with love, courage, and faith, we can rise above any obstacle and create beauty from every challenge.

From deep within, before logic takes hold, there's a knowing women have, our intuition. Too often, Latinas are taught to doubt it, to wait for proof or permission. But our foremothers didn't wait. Without degrees or resources, they trusted their hands, their prayers, and the voice inside. They were healers, protectors, and teachers who wrapped us in faith and whispered strength into our bones.

This story is for them—and for every woman reclaiming her voice, every mother breaking cycles, and every girl who was told "you can't" and chose to rise anyway. It's for anyone walking the path to purpose—imperfectly but boldly—day by day.

TWO PHRASES THAT MADE ME

Two truths have shaped my life.

The first came from my mother, who was a teacher who graduated from the University of Puerto Rico. She said it, not once, not occasionally, but almost daily: "Never depend on anyone to survive financially. The only way for a woman to do it is through education." She wove these words into our days—while brushing my hair, cooking arroz con habichuelas, or folding laundry. It was always present.

"Look at your dad and me," she would say. "If he left tomorrow, what would I do if I didn't have a degree?" As a little girl, I said, "But he loves you." She'd respond, "Love can disappear in a second. You need to stand on your own."

That became my foundation. Education wasn't for prestige—it was my survival plan.

The second phrase came from my father, who also held his Juris Doctor degree, regardless of how he earned his GED after turning 18 while serving in the military during World War II. He would say it quietly, steadily, and forcefully: "Apuesto a ti." — I bet on you.

He never said much, but when he did, it carried weight. My father had lived through hardship—losing his father at 12, caring for his sisters and mother as head of household since then, and serving in WWII, with quiet strength. He showed love through action with early mornings, warm breakfasts, and steady hands. When he said, I bet on you, I felt it in my bones. His belief in me became my anchor. Whenever the world made me question my worth, I returned to his voice—and believed in myself again.

To this day, those words are a shield against fear. They ground me in truth, courage, and the reminder that my purpose is non-negotiable.

MY MOTHER'S LEGACY: IMPERFECT STRENGTH

My mother, Gladys Román Quiles, experienced eras of candles and smart speakers, from handwritten letters to asking Alexa for Bad Bunny. She was the first in our family to attend college, became a nurse residence supervisor, and then went on to become a beloved fourth-grade teacher. Her students mourned at her funeral, remembering how she transformed their lives.

But my mother also lived with manic depression. Some days she cooked, prayed, and folded laundry with quiet care. Other days, she withdrew into silence or storms. I learned to read her moods, stay small, and adapt. Still, her example taught me how to endure. She showed me that resilience isn't just about pushing forward—it's about surviving the day, showing up with trembling hands, whispering prayers over your children even when you feel broken.

Though her instability prompted me to leave home early, it also shaped my strength. In her daily rituals, I found discipline. In her love of language, I found my voice. Her contradictions became my foundation: that you can be imperfect and still powerful. That even amid struggle, you can sow the seeds of a different, joyful life.

MY FATHER'S STORY: PROVIDER, PROTECTOR, PATRIOT

My father passed away in 2003. A World War II veteran, he was disciplined, loyal, and deeply present. At 12, he stepped into manhood. His father died, and he had to take on raising his four sisters and supporting his mother. He later earned his GED, a bachelor's in business, and a law degree from the University of Puerto Rico.

He married at 35 and became a father at 36. He never raised his voice. He didn't have to. His presence spoke louder.

He woke us early, made us breakfast, and made sure we felt safe. He decided to become a college professor after retiring as the Director of the Botanical Garden at the University of Puerto Rico. He believed that working and helping others through his example and teachings was part of his life until the end, and that is precisely how it happened. His death occurred on November 4, and he had worked continuously for more than 60 years until August of that same year.

When he told me, *Apuesto a ti*, it wasn't flattery. It was a promise. He had weighed the world and believed with all the trust in his heart that I could make something extraordinary of it. His belief became my fire.

He also showed me what fatherhood could look like. He was tender without being soft. He was firm without being cruel. He listened more than he lectured. And he worked hard—not just at his job, but at being a steady presence in our lives.

In many ways, he laid the blueprint for the kind of person I strive to be: consistent, values-driven, and someone who follows through on her commitments. Not perfect. Just steady. And that, to me, matters more than anything else.

A PROM DRESS AND A VOLVO

UMass Amherst had always been my dream, but it felt out of reach. My middle-class Puerto Rican parents couldn't afford out-of-state tuition. Still, I kept acting and taking steps toward making it happen, as if it were already possible. I wasn't sure how it would happen, but I knew it would, and I had to be prepared.

What drew me to UMass wasn't just the idea of leaving the island—it was the promise of opportunity. In Puerto Rico, people often said you needed palas—connections—to get ahead. Without them, doors stayed closed no matter how hard you worked. However, a degree from a U.S. university, especially one with a strong reputation like the University of Massachusetts Amherst, holds significant value. It meant credibility. It meant being seen. It meant that my effort could finally speak louder than my last name or who I knew.

I still remember the day UMass recruiters visited my high school, University Gardens. They spoke about access and possibility, and they stayed after the presentation to help students complete their applications. No one had ever done that before. For the first time, I felt seen—not just as a student from the island, but as someone with potential that reached beyond it.

So yes, UMass was a dream—but more than that, it was a door. A way to claim my independence, to honor my parents' sacrifices, and to prove that a girl without palas could still build her own path.

Then something extraordinary happened.

While shopping for prom shoes, my dad ran into a friend who told him he'd heard his name on a local game show. He had entered a sweepstakes and forgotten. He won—a brand-new Volvo. He sold it for $63,000 and asked me, *Do you want to study in the U.S.?* Yes, I said. No hesitation. And that, yes, changed everything.

That moment taught me that life makes room for your purpose when you stay ready. Miracles are real when you believe in your path and purpose, and that you need to be prepared for when the doors open. That one unexpected win changed my trajectory—not because it made everything easy, but because it made it possible. My father turned a lucky break into a life-changing opportunity.

BECOMING MYSELF IN A NEW LAND

At the age of 18, I moved to Massachusetts. My writing and comprehension in English were strong. My speech and being able to understand what people would say to me, especially when it came to idiomatic expressions and slang. Not so much.

I recorded every lecture. Transcribed each one and studied late. My first semester, I earned a 4.0. Eventually, I earned three degrees, including a Ph.D. in Hispanic American Literature. I got married at 29. Became a mother at 31. And came out as queer at 36.

But then, life unraveled. I lost custody of my daughters for eleven years. My ex-husband had one of the most powerful lawyers in town—someone known for influencing the judge assigned to my case. That same judge was later disrobed for the very injustices she had inflicted on countless other mothers like me.

I still believe what happened was the result of a deeply flawed and corrupt legal system—one that punishes those without financial privilege. Coming from Puerto Rico, where custody is rarely taken from a mother unless she is a convicted felon or battling addiction, I couldn't imagine that love, stability, and integrity wouldn't be enough. I was naive. I thought truth would prevail without a lawyer. I was wrong.

The years that followed were hollowed by absence. I missed birthdays, first dances, and goodnight kisses. I cried in bathroom stalls. I carried heartbreak like a second skin—a wound so deep I once believed I might never recover.

Still, I didn't stop. I rebuilt. I kept moving.

During those years, I redefined what it meant to be a mother. I mothered through emails and phone calls. Through prayers. Through hope. I mothered by becoming someone they would be proud to come back to.

And when they did, I didn't just welcome them. I welcomed the chance to mother again—with more honesty, with more healing, with more of myself reclaimed.

During those years, I also mentored young women—many of them single mothers, first-generation college students, or women navigating heartbreak and self-doubt. They came to me through my classes, community groups, and sometimes by word of mouth. I saw in them the same hunger to rise, the same exhaustion from carrying too much alone.

I shared my story not to seek pity, but to offer proof that survival is possible. I helped them write personal statements, prepare for interviews, and reclaim their voices after a period of silence. I reminded them that their past did not define their worth, and that healing was not a detour—it was part of the work.

In mentoring them, I was also mentoring myself. Every time I told a young woman, 'You can start again,' I believed it a little more for myself, too. I wrote, taught, and became a mirror for those who needed to see their strength reflected to them. My story spoke louder than my shame or anger at a broken court system.

I learned that transformation doesn't always come from success; it often blooms from pain. And in the rebuilding, we find out who we truly are.

FOR THE GIRLS WHO DON'T YET KNOW THEIR POWER

To every girl who has known shame, silence, or scarcity:

I see you.

To every queer Boricua still finding her voice:

I honor you.

To every daughter of a tired mother who still tried:

I believe in you.

And more than that: Apuesto a ti.

You are not here by accident. You are not surviving by luck. You are thriving by destiny.

You come from women who created medicine from plants, healing from prayer, and strength from nothing.

So, walk as if their prayers still carry you—because they do.

You are part of a legacy bigger than your fear. You are the continuation of their dream.

You don't need to wait to feel ready. Your ancestors are already walking beside you.

And when you rise, remember, you're not just growing for yourself. You're rising for every girl watching, wondering if she's allowed to shine.

A LEGACY TO LIVE BY

Now, with both my parents gone, I live by the truths they gave me:

Be self-sufficient.

Apuesto a ti.

At 55, I am still writing my story. It's not flashy. It's not perfect. But it's mine. And it is enough.

My purpose is clear: To rise—and to lift others as I do.

To the next woman who doubts herself, trust your voice. Bet on your dream. Say yes when the universe opens the door.

Say yes to what is to come, *apostando en ti.*

Always.

ADVICE THAT CHANGED MY LIFE

One of the most powerful pieces of advice a mentor gave me was, "Don't wait for permission to walk in your purpose." As a Puerto Rican woman in education, I often found myself in spaces where I felt I had to overprove my worth. But those words reminded me that I carry the legacy of ancestors who moved with purpose despite barriers. That advice still guides me—primarily when I advocate for families, stand firm in leadership, or write my truth.

A piece of advice I give to others is: *Always bet on yourself.* When systems fail you, doors close, or doubt sneaks in—go back to what you know. Every big decision in my life, from leaving unhealthy situations to speaking up in boardrooms, has required me to believe in my value before anyone else did. Never let impostor syndrome take over your true self. That self-trust has changed and will continue to change everything you set your heart and mind to.

Biography

Déborah L. González, Ph.D., is a Puerto Rican-born educator, writer, and lifelong advocate for cultural reclamation, language equity, and community healing. She holds a Ph.D. in Hispanic American Literature from the University of Massachusetts Amherst. She has spent over 25 years advancing the rights and dignity of Latinx, multilingual, and historically marginalized communities in both K–12 and higher education.

A former actress for Telemundo Puerto Rico, Déborah transformed her early passion for storytelling into a distinguished academic and public service career. She has served as a university professor, playwright, keynote speaker, and, most recently, as a public education leader in Worcester, Massachusetts, where she co-developed a districtwide Family and Community Engagement Framework. Her expertise spans language access compliance, family-school partnerships, and bilingual curriculum design.

Her writing is profoundly shaped by her journey as a queer Latina mother, a daughter shaped by generational sacrifice, and a woman rebuilding her legacy through voice. Whether mentoring young educators, reclaiming Boricua traditions with her daughters, or crafting essays that uplift silenced stories, Déborah centers intuition, resilience, and radical love as tools of liberation.

Through her words, she invites others—especially Latinas—to honor their lineage, lead with truth, and bet on themselves.

Déborah L. González
gonzalezdl@worcesterschools.net

BECOMING IN THE UNBECOMING

DULCE OROZCO

"I choose presence over perfection, connection over control."

DEDICATION

To Hiroko,

Thank you for a lifelong loving friendship, and thank you for everything your beautiful soul continues to teach me every day.

A wise coach often reminded me, "Pain is unavoidable, but suffering is optional." As human beings, we will all experience pain, which is simply a part of life. However, many of us inflict or perpetuate this pain by dwelling on it in our minds, and this can invite and intensify the suffering. When this mindset becomes our default, suffering lingers and feels hard to shake.

Being a psychotherapist offers me the gift of seeing people up close, getting to know their deep and private fears and feelings. My specialty is working with Latina leaders and women of color from immigrant families. I have observed a common experience: being extremely hard on ourselves to the point of setting the stage where automatic thoughts list every mistake and failure, dwelling on them, and quickly ignoring what is working. As you can imagine, this background can create the perfect storm and easily lead to getting stuck in these difficult, painful places.

These past few months have been exceptionally challenging for me. I have intentionally worked, with the help of therapists, coaches, friends, and family, to stay away from the sticky place where suffering is the norm. This book is scheduled to be released on the first anniversary of the day my dear friend passed away. We met in kindergarten in Venezuela; our birthdays were one day apart, and over the years, she became like family.

We shared 37 years of life together and losing her unexpectedly from childbirth complications has been my biggest lesson on how life can change course from the plans we make. I pictured my life with her by my side, and I am learning to manage my closest experience with death while letting go of this idea of "how it was meant to be."

I can't help but give meaning to this synchronicity. In Spanish, I love the word *diosidencia,* a made-up word that combines *coincidencia* and God. To me, the fact that the book was released on the day it was is a sign.

Being a part of this beautiful book, which tells the stories of incredible, talented, creative, innovative, kind, extraordinary, resilient, trailblazing, nurturing, wise, authentic, and passionate Latinas, is a gift. I've had the luxury of knowing many of the authors who made this book possible. Over the years, creating and nurturing connections with mentors/friends who look like me has been instrumental, as they have shown me what is possible and modeled how to be myself. Opening doors for others has become the most loving way I know to move forward.

Seeing this has been helpful in my journey of embracing and welcoming parts of myself that I used to ignore or avoid, as it encourages me to be myself and let go of the idea of what I should be.

If you are struggling to embrace what is, because it doesn't look anything like what you had in mind, or if you are struggling to accept and welcome parts of yourself that you don't particularly like or have been trying to ignore in the past, I hope this helps you. I spent so much time fixating on one door, waiting for it to open, that I missed the windows that were always open along the way. To find joy in what I have, and during the process of accepting and embracing my whole self, expanding my capacity for flexibility and learning to create more space have been crucial in gaining a new perspective. I have learned that for me, being very rigid about how things should look does not work. Don't get me wrong, I am not saying that visualizing what you want and having clear goals and objectives is not helpful, by any means. In fact, I try to do it in my own way. However, sticking to that one way and expecting that result has not been helpful to me. As clichéd as it sounds, this rigidity has kept me from seeing easier, kinder paths forward.

In a way, I can understand where this idea comes from. I was born and raised in Venezuela and came to the United States at the age of 17. That romanticized view included believing everything here was better and thinking following what most people did was the right path. This, in a way, taught me to look at that one door and that door only; in reality, I am now able to see that it was never the door for me.

I heard from someone that expectation equals suffering. I realized that in my case, my extremely high expectations, especially when it came to myself, were all the "shoulds" and a very fixed, perfect idea of what my life should look like. They thrived in that sticky, rigid place. There is only one "good way to do things," and this place bans accepting and loving the parts of myself that are challenging for me and is anti-living in the present; therefore, it creates the perfect environment for suffering not only to survive but flourish.

I grew up being a good student. In my house, academics were highly valued and growing up in a middle-class family where both of my parents were university professors, the idea of not attending college was unthinkable. I suppose my parents grew accustomed to me being a good student, and I did too. At some point, not only did I expect this of myself, but I also forgot to appreciate it. Therefore, not only was I expected to be a good student, but I was also expected to excel in everything.

The expectations I had of myself were so unachievable that it reached the point where, a few years ago, hearing a compliment about my work was highly uncomfortable, especially after events or workshops when some people stayed to say hi and thank me. As you can imagine, and if you are one of those people (I am), most of the time you genuinely want to connect, express gratitude, or share some commonalities, or what came up for you. I know because I have done this many times in the past. And yet, whenever I was the recipient of those kind words, not only did I feel uncomfortable, but all my insecurities came to the surface because I didn't believe them. There was a part of me that even thought they were saying it out of pity. Naturally, this is not sustainable or tolerable, so I ultimately felt like "a failure in most areas of my life."

Pause for a moment: Are you holding yourself to a standard that no one else is even asking for?

Recently, I went to see the corpse flower bloom, a rare event that happens every 7–10 years, lasts only 24 hours, and emits a smell reminiscent of rotten meat. Watching this flower up close and seeing people waiting in line excitedly to see it made me think about how everyone completely embraced its uniqueness, even if they had to cover their noses due to the smell. Its colossal size, its weird, almost fictional shape, and its short duration came with one rotten (literally) element, which was the way it smelled. While I was there, I thought about why I can't feel good about myself and all those parts of me that are "smelly" like this magnificent flower? What if I could take it all in and even practice living with curiosity towards these parts of myself that I've been trying to hide and have been ashamed of because of how unconventional they are? If people can admire a flower with a fierce, unforgettable scent—full of wonder despite its smell—can you start to admire the parts of yourself that feel messy, loud, or misunderstood?

In a way, this is what I have been trying to do these past few months. I have attempted not only to change my relationship with those parts of myself that I've tried to ignore or avoid, but also to acknowledge them. This has been particularly challenging because I am still dealing with the significant loss of my friend who passed, and the current situation in the United States can be very energy-consuming and disheartening, so at times it feels that I do not have what it takes to go through it all at once.

I know that I am not alone in my work as a Latina immigrant therapist, and sharing my experience with other business owners, I have seen how conditioned we are to present ourselves perfectly. Once again, I can understand where this pressure comes from, but I also understand firsthand the price that we pay because of it.

During this journey of learning how to be in a relationship with these parts of myself, I have opened up a whole new world of love and connection. For me, community has been a massive part of all of this. Seeing people like me this applies to many levels: physical appearance, those who sound like me, do similar work, and do what I've been afraid of doing modeling what can be done and how it can be done differently from a place of alignment and authenticity has been priceless. Many of these connections have evolved into friendships, allies, and people I can consider part of my support network.

Since I didn't have these kinds of mentorships, this is still a relatively new experience for me—one I deeply value, especially when I think about my daughters and how I want them to have this support from an early age. This is also why I care so deeply about collaborating with and supporting programs for Black and Brown girls and young adults. Organizations that create safe, affirming, and empowering spaces for them are doing transformational work, and I've witnessed that impact up close. My daughters have benefited from these kinds of programs, and it has left me feeling profoundly grateful. The sense of visibility, encouragement, and joy they've received has stayed with them—and with me. I invite others to support and uplift these organizations in whatever way they can, because their ripple effect is powerful and lasting.

Opening up to myself has not been an easy and always joyful journey, but luckily, the universe has placed the right people along the way exactly when I needed them. Having this support has been life-changing.

Due to the current situation in the United States, I am in the process of reshaping my business, and I am uncertain about its future direction. Losing my friend in the way that it happened has also been a vivid reminder of how quickly everything can change and how important it is to be able to adapt and embrace the change. This is something I have always done as a therapist. However, on a personal level, I am now doing it differently because part of embracing and intentionally letting go of all the heartfelt "shoulds" has allowed me to be with those parts of myself that I've been avoiding over the years, while learning that they've always been there patiently waiting for me to acknowledge them.

As you read this, I invite you to ask yourself: What does "being more you" look like today, not forever, just today?

I am still in the process of learning how to show up more authentically every day. I know this is a lifelong process, and I will need help, support, inspiration, community, guidance, and so much more. I also know that there will be ups and downs and that none of that will take away the progress I've made or everything I have learned so far.

I choose presence over perfection, and connection over control—today, and every day, I can.

Special dedication and thank you to, Hiroko, for a lifelong loving friendship, and thank you for everything your beautiful soul continues to teach me every day.

ADVICE THAT CHANGED MY LIFE

When I think about advice that changed my life, I don't recall one single phrase that transformed everything. Instead, I think of how many people have shared the same message with me in different ways and moments. Many have been women of color and Latinas, like myself, examples of what I aspire to embody. Though their words might have sounded different each time, the essence was the same: Be yourself. Embrace yourself. When you do, opportunities will come your way.

I now understand and appreciate this advice on a deeper level. It's not just something to remember, it's a way of living, an ongoing practice. Honoring this wisdom often means seeking support. I've learned that I sometimes need the care of therapists, coaches, mentors, friends, and loved ones. Seeing myself through their eyes and noticing how they accept me fully, helps me appreciate myself even more.

I'm deeply grateful for their support and for how grounded and authentic I feel when I apply this advice. It's not always easy to show up as ourselves, but I hope you give yourself permission to do so a little more each day. And remember, "you don't have to do it alone."

Biography

Dulce Orozco is a proud Venezuelan immigrant, licensed mental health counselor, speaker, and mom who supports women of color—especially first-generation Latinx daughters—in reclaiming their power by shedding the weight of expectation and embracing self-compassion.

Rooted in her own story of migration and healing, Dulce understands the complexities of carrying cultural legacies, generational responsibilities, and personal grief. She creates supportive spaces where women can unpack these burdens with courage, find their voices, and nurture their whole selves.

With experience in private practice, community mental health, psychiatric hospitals, and youth education, Dulce blends clinical insight with cultural wisdom and lived experience. She has shared her work with organizations like Google, the Broad Institute, Merrimack College, the City of Cambridge, Chica Project, and Love Your Magic.

Dulce was honored as an Amplify Latinx 2023 Honoree, named one of Latina Center Maria's Inspirational Women of 2024, and recognized as an ALX 100 Honoree for 2025. Fluent in Spanish, English, and Portuguese, she lives in Massachusetts with her two daughters who teach her daily to choose presence over perfection.

For Dulce, liberation begins the moment we choose to love ourselves fully and without apology.

Dulce Orozco

dulce.orozco.lmhc@gmail.com

Instagram: @latinaimmigranttherapist

www.dulceorozco.com

HOLDING THE DOOR OPEN

EVELYN A. TONEY

"I am my ancestors' wildest dreams—and my children's greatest example."

DEDICATION

For my mother, whose strength built the foundation I stand on; my husband, whose love and faith have been my anchor; and my children—Makhai, Javen, and Thomas—may you always remember that strength runs in your veins and possibility has no limits

I grew up in Plumley Village, a housing complex in Worcester, Massachusetts, where the walls were thin, the struggles were loud, and hope had to be held onto tightly. My mother, a single mom of three, worked harder than anyone I've ever known. By day, she worked factory jobs earning $2 an hour. By night, she cleaned banks—sometimes taking my brothers and me along on school nights to help vacuum, dust, and empty trash cans. She did all this while learning English, determined to create a better life for her children.

Our community was our lifeline. In Plumley, families looked out for one another. If one neighbor had extra bread, another had milk, and someone else had rice, we'd pool it together so everyone ate. It wasn't charity; it was survival, and it taught me that collective strength is more powerful than any single person's struggle.

Girls Inc. of Worcester was our first safe haven—a place where I could dream beyond our immediate reality. I would bring my younger brothers along because my mom had no childcare options. But as we got older, to keep us together, we joined the Boys & Girls Club. It became another anchor in our lives, giving us structure, mentors, and a sense of belonging.

I remember being nine years old, with my brothers Willy, who was eight, and Mike, who was six, there was a small store inside the club. We were so hungry, but we had no money for snacks. That day, Willy and I decided we weren't going to sit hungry. We found scraps of paper, folded them into airplanes, and colored them to make them look special. We sold them for five cents each, determined to make enough for all three of us to have something to eat. It wasn't much, but it was ours—earned with creativity and grit.

Looking back, I realize that was the moment entrepreneurship first took root in me. We weren't just kids making paper airplanes; we were problem-solvers. And maybe it's no surprise that years later, Willy would own two barber shops and other businesses, and Mike would become a master barber. That day taught us all that no matter how little you start with, you can create something out of nothing.

Eventually, my mother enrolled in beauty school. After graduating, she began working as a stylist at Smart Cuts Plus. She wasn't the owner then—just a stylist with a dream and a work ethic that couldn't be ignored. Her boss saw her passion and promoted her to manager. I remember that time in our lives vividly, because it was the first time we could buy clothes from a real department store. We still did layaways, but after years of only knowing thrift stores and donations, it felt like a turning point.

Then came the opportunity that changed everything. Her boss offered to sell her the salon for $10,000. My mom only had $300 in her bank account. But her faith was stronger than her fear, and her boss believed in her so much that he made a deal: she could pay him monthly until it was paid off. My mom was so determined that she made weekly payments instead. Within one year, she owned Smart Cuts Plus outright.

That was forty years ago. She became the first Latina to own a hair salon on Main South in Worcester—a trailblazer who showed me that leadership isn't just about titles or positions; it's about grit, faith, and never closing the door behind you. Working there alongside my brothers, sweeping floors, and greeting customers, I learned my first lessons in business and leadership from the best boss I've ever had.

I didn't just watch my mother build a business; I worked right alongside her. From the time I was old enough to hold a broom, I was sweeping hair, folding towels, booking appointments, and eventually learning to do hair myself. For years, I styled clients, knowing that every haircut was more than just a service; it was a way to connect, to listen, and to help people feel seen and confident.

Like my mother, I was no stranger to long days and late nights. I often worked two or three jobs at a time, not because it was easy, but because it was necessary. I always had a side hustle—whether it was hair, retail, or other part-time work—and every role taught me something new about people, persistence, and possibility.

Eventually, I opened my own business—Plants Flower Shop, Unique Treasures and Gifts—a combination flower shop and antique store located right next door to my mother's salon. I managed the shop while still taking hair clients in between, all while raising my son as a single mother and working toward my bachelor's degree in business management. That time in my life was exhausting, but it was also empowering. I was determined to better my life for my son, just as my mother had done for me.

In the early 2000s, the flower shop industry began to shift dramatically with the rise of 1-800-Flowers and big-box retailers entering the market. Business slowed, and I was faced with a hard decision. Many people let pride keep them in situations that no longer serve them, but I didn't care what others would think. I cared that I was smart enough to know when it was time to close one chapter and prepare for the next.

Closing the shop wasn't failure; it was a strategic move. That decision freed me to step into an entirely new career path—one that would change everything. I was offered an opportunity in the mortgage lending world, and I took it.

My career began as a mortgage loan officer, where I discovered the life-changing power of homeownership and access to credit. I worked my way up to Director-level underwriting roles, mastering the complexities of lending and building a reputation for integrity and results.

Breaking into the industry wasn't easy. I was often the only Latina in the room, and in a space dominated by men, I had to prove myself twice over. There were people who underestimated me before I even spoke. Some thought I was "too nice" to make it in business, but I turned that into my strength. My clients didn't just see me as a banker or loan officer; they saw me as someone who genuinely cared about their future.

I built my career on relationships, trust, and the belief that financial literacy is power. Over time, those relationships opened new opportunities. I stepped into leadership roles, became a realtor, and joined the boards of organizations that aligned with my values: Adelante Worcester, the Latino Education Institute, NAHREP Central Massachusetts, the Latin American Business Organization, Girls Inc. of Worcester and the Massachusetts Women of Color Coalition (MAWOCC).

The turning point for me was realizing that I wasn't just building my own career; I was becoming the person who could open doors for others. I had walked through plenty of doors that someone else unlocked for me, but now it was my turn to be the one with the keys.

Today, I carry my mother's legacy in every role I hold—as Vice President of Business and Community Development at Bay State Savings Bank, a realtor, and a board member for organizations that reflect my values. I currently serve as Vice President of NAHREP Central Massachusetts and will proudly step into the role of President in February 2026.

My career has given me a front-row seat to the transformative power of opportunity. I've seen what happens when someone finally hears "yes" after a lifetime of hearing "no." I've watched families close on their first home, small business owners secure the funding to grow, and women step into leadership positions they once thought were out of reach. Each of those moments reminds me of my own journey—from Plumley Village to the boardroom—and fuels my commitment to making sure I am never the last.

I mentor women, especially women of color, because I know how isolating it can feel to be the only one in the room. I speak openly about my upbringing, my failures, and my pivots because I want others to understand that setbacks aren't the end of the story; they're often the beginning of a better chapter.

Leadership, to me, is about access. It's about making sure that when I step into a space, I don't just hold the door open—I make sure it stays open long enough for others to walk through with confidence. It's about leveraging my position to connect people to resources, information, and networks they might not otherwise have.

I think about my three children often in this work. They've seen me juggle late nights, back-to-back commitments, and a calendar full of community events, but they've also seen me show up—not just for myself, but for my community. My hope is that when they look back, they'll understand that success isn't just measured by titles or income, but by the number of lives you've impacted along the way.

I am my mother's daughter—resilient, determined, and unafraid to take risks. I am also my own woman—a leader, a door-opener, and a believer in the power of faith and kindness to change the world. My story started in a small housing complex in Worcester, but it will never end there. I am an ELLA Poderosa, and I am just getting started.

ADVICE THAT CHANGED MY LIFE

Early in my lending career, a trusted manager once told me I was "too nice for this business." At first, that sounded like criticism—but I quickly realized it was actually a challenge to lead differently. I decided to lean into my kindness, to make empathy and trust the foundation of every relationship I built. That mindset not only shaped my leadership style but also became the driving force behind my career growth—from mortgage loan officer to Director of Underwriting, and now to executive leadership. It's proof that you can lead with heart and still achieve excellence.

Another piece of wisdom that continues to guide me is simple yet powerful: *don't let pride keep you stuck.* When my flower-and-antique business faced growing competition, I made the difficult decision to close that chapter and start a new one. It wasn't failure—it was wisdom. Knowing when to pivot allows you to seize new opportunities with clarity and courage. Change doesn't mean defeat; it means growth. And often, the courage to shift directions becomes the key to your next breakthrough.

Biography

Evelyn A. Toney is the Vice President of Business and Community Development at Bay State Bank, a Realtor, and a passionate advocate for women of color in business and leadership.

Born and raised in Worcester, Massachusetts, Evelyn grew up in Plumley Village, a housing community that taught her perseverance, purpose, and faith. Inspired by her mother—the first Latina to own a salon on Main South—Evelyn built her life around hard work, community impact, and breaking barriers.

Determined to create a better future, she balanced multiple jobs while pursuing her Business Management degree and launching her first boutique. Her journey of resilience and self-belief shaped the leader she is today.

Evelyn went on to excel in the mortgage and banking industries, rising from Loan Officer to executive leadership. Known for her integrity, empathy, and results-driven approach, she now helps individuals, families, and entrepreneurs access the financial tools to build lasting wealth.

She serves as Vice President of NAHREP Central Massachusetts (incoming President 2026) and sits on the boards of LABO, LEI, Girls Inc. of Worcester, Adelante Worcester, and MAWOCC. Evelyn is currently pursuing her MBA at the American College of Education, graduating in 2026, continuing her lifelong commitment to growth, leadership, and service.

Evelyn and her husband have built a life grounded in faith, perseverance, and love as they raise their three children and continue to uplift their community.

Her guiding mantra: "Faith made me fearless, perseverance made me unstoppable."

Evelyn Toney

etoney@baystatebank.com

www.EvelynToney.com

https://linkedin.com/in/evelyn-a-toney-676b0859

FROM EL BATEY TO WORKING FOR A
CONGRESSMAN: EMBRACING MY INNER
PODEROSA

GLADYS RODRIGUEZ-PARKER

"Because neither today, nor tomorrow, nor ever, will our homeland cease to be ours."
— **Eugenio María de Hostos**

DEDICATION

For My Husband Steve, my sons Carlos & Jonathan and my Jibara family!

What does it mean to rise from fire? To have your childhood home destroyed in flames of hate, only to one day walk the halls of Congress. This is not only my story—it is the story of resilience, survival, and triumph for an entire people.

This chapter is more than a personal journey—it is a testament to resilience, faith, and service. It tells of a Jibara girl, born on the mainland during the migrant season but raised in the mountains of Puerto Rico, whose life was shaped by migration, fire, prejudice, and perseverance. It is a story of how hardship can forge strength, how motherhood can inspire determination, and how service can become a calling that transforms not only one possession, but entire communities. From the Batey of Cerro Gordo to the halls of political power, this is the story of embracing one's **Poderosa**—an unstoppable force rooted in culture, faith, and unyielding courage.

BEGINNINGS IN PUERTO RICO

Some stories are born from comfort; mine was born from fire. To understand the woman who would one day work for a congressman, you must first picture a barefoot girl running through the hills of Puerto Rico, carrying both the joy of her mountains and the weight of a world that told her she did not belong. This is not just my story—it is the story of thousands of Puerto Ricans, U.S. citizens who migrated to the mainland, who navigated oceans of prejudice, language, and doubt, and still dared to rise.

I was born on the mainland during a migrant season, but I grew up in Puerto Rico. I was raised in Cerro Gordo, San Lorenzo, where tradition was not simply remembered but lived. My parents were Jíbaros, descendants of Taíno, African, and Spanish ancestry. They worked the land with hands calloused by survival, yet hearts full of resilience. From them, I inherited stubborn strength and cultural pride that became my armor. That strength, like an ember, would carry me through storms to come.

MIGRATION AND SURVIVAL IN BOSTON

By 1969, agriculture could no longer sustain us, and U.S. policies like the Jones Act further limited economic growth and trade opportunities on the island. My family of ten migrated north, trading green mountains for gray cityscapes, the sweet scent of earth for the sharp stench of diesel. We arrived in South Boston in winter, seeing snow for the first time—white, cold, fleeting, like the illusion of belonging.

We moved into the D Street Projects, a neighborhood boiling with racial hostility. South Boston in the late '60s and '70s was a battlefield. Dominated by gangs like Bulger's Winter Hill crew, it demanded whiteness and punished brown skin. Going to school, attending church, or buying bread meant risking harassment, slurs, or violence. Words like "spic" and "nigger" cut deeper than Boston's cold winds.

On New Year's Eve of 1969, hatred burst through our windows. As we gathered to welcome the year, Molotov cocktails rained into our home. Flames swallowed the walls while smoke choked the air. We fled into the freezing night with nothing but each other, leaving our possessions, including all of our Christmas presents, to burn.

For a child, this loss carried a deeper wound. In Puerto Rican tradition, the holidays did not end on December 25th— they reached their peak on January 6th with Three Kings Day, when children placed grass under their beds for the Magi's camels and woke to gifts symbolizing hope and faith. To lose our presents just days before that sacred celebration felt like having joy itself stolen from us. The fire robbed us not only of toys, but also of a ritual that connected us to our culture, leaving a hollow ache I carry to this day.

That night scarred me, but it also steeled me. Survival meant refusing to let hatred define me. That fire became my compass, pointing me toward a life of service and advocacy, and later stood in stark contrast to the triumph I would achieve nearly three decades later.

EDUCATION AND MOTHERHOOD

Boston forced me to grow fast. English became my lifeline. While in junior high and high school, a kid like me had to battle daily for acceptance against the backdrop of racial turmoil, struggling to carve out a place in classrooms divided by prejudice and fear. I became my family's interpreter, translating at schools, hospitals, and stores. Every new word was a weapon, a step toward empowerment.

As the first in my family to graduate from high school, I carried the hopes of generations. At seventeen, I became a mother. Many assumed that was the end of my story, but my son Carlos became my reason to fight harder.

In 1975, I entered the University of Massachusetts at Amherst as a young, single mother. Professors and classmates doubted me. Could a Jibara girl with an accent and a baby succeed here? I answered yes. I woke before dawn to feed Carlos, pushed his stroller across campus with books stacked high, and studied while rocking his cradle. My diploma proved Puerto Rican women, young mothers, and migrants belonged in every room. More importantly, those years taught me the discipline of balancing impossible loads. When I doubted myself, I remembered a mentor's words: *"Never let anyone else define your worth."*

That advice helped me push through doors others tried to close. Those early school battles for acceptance became training for the boardrooms and political arenas where I would again face doubt and prejudice, but this time with sharper tools and stronger resolve.

ENTERING PUBLIC SERVICE

The professional world tested me again. In boardrooms where I was the only Latina, my accent was questioned, my confidence dismissed, my heritage treated as a flaw. Every slight became fuel.

When Jim McGovern was elected to Congress in 1996, he asked me to serve as his District Director. On January 3, 1997, I became the first Puerto Rican woman in Massachusetts history to hold such a role, breaking barriers and setting a precedent for others to follow. That milestone became a beacon for younger generations, showing them that our presence belonged not just in the room but at the table of decision-making. The backlash was immediate. Calls flooded McGovern's parents' home: *"Why did Jimmy hire that spic?"* But I showed up every day, head high, carrying not only my own dignity but that of my community.

The irony was not lost on me: on New Year's Eve of 1969, my family was nearly destroyed by Molotov cocktails thrown through our windows in South Boston, and just two days after New Year's Eve of 1997, I stood as the first Puerto Rican woman in Massachusetts history to hold such a role, and one of the most powerful Puerto Rican women in the state, sworn in as District Director to a member of Congress. The fire meant to erase us instead forged my resolve and led me to this moment of triumph.

Working for a Congressman was both an honor and a responsibility. I managed his connection to the district: fielding calls from constituents in crisis, mediating between federal agencies and families, and ensuring migrants, working-class families, and underrepresented voices were heard in Washington.

One moment stands out. When a group of Latina grandmothers spoke about raising their grandchildren due to substance abuse in their families. Their words mirrored my own family's challenges. I worked with them and community leaders to create the Hector Reyes Rehabilitation House, offering dignity and recovery to men leaving prison. That work reminded me again of my mother's advice—that service must always be love put into action.

POLITICS AND NATIONAL SERVICE

My work expanded to the national stage. I campaigned for Al Gore, John Kerry, Hillary Clinton, and Barack Obama. Campaign life was exhausting but electric. Each voter reminded me democracy lives not in marble halls but in neighborhoods and conversations.

Politics is not just about the presidency. It is about city councils, school committees, and grassroots fights that shape daily life. I dedicated myself to connecting communities with power: registering voters, translating ballots, ensuring no one was silenced by language barriers. Democracy breathes strongest when ordinary people find their voice.

Campaigns were not only about winning elections—they were about showing young Puerto Ricans, Latinas, and other marginalized youth that their voices mattered, that they had the right to lead, and that our legacy would only grow stronger if they carried it forward.

At every step, I leaned on the mentor's words that had guided me since my youth: *"Never let anyone else define your worth."* In politics, as in life, those words carried me forward.

A LIFE OF SERVICE

My journey has not been without scars. I have lost loved ones, questioned my worth, and carried the sting of slurs. But doubt is powerless when you return to your roots—the Jibara child running barefoot in Puerto Rico, the young mother pushing a stroller through college, the Puerto Rican woman working for a congressman.

I embraced my inner **Poderosa**—the unstoppable force no prejudice could extinguish. Service became the thread through every chapter of my life. Whether advocating for tenants, guiding young Latinas, or helping struggling families, service was not a duty but a calling. Leadership is measured not by titles, but by the possessions you lift along the way. Our struggles, though heavy, are laced with triumph. We are not invisible. We are not voiceless. We are here, and we belong. Every time I extended my hand to help another, I remembered: Service is love in action.

Every chapter of my life has been a climb—from mountains to city streets, from classrooms to the offices of government. Along the way, I carried the weight of a homeland constrained by outdated policies and colonial status, the same forces that pushed my parents to leave Puerto Rico in search of survival. That legacy became fuel, proof that even when a people are displaced, their children can rise, reclaim dignity, and fight for justice.

My service has taught me that leadership is love in action— whether fighting for a constituent's benefits, standing with families battling addiction, or mentoring young women. Power is never meant to be hoarded; it is meant to be shared, multiplied, and handed forward. Service, for me, is not an act performed in spare hours but a way of breathing, a compass guiding every step. It is the fire that carried me from a burning apartment in Boston to the halls of influence, the quiet strength that grounds me in community, and the faith that tomorrow can be better than today.

If there is one truth I carry, it is this: No matter where we begin, our voices can rise, our power can grow, and our presence can never again be denied. The arc of my journey—from Molotov cocktails hurled into our home on New Year's Eve 1969 to being sworn in just after New Year's 1997 as District Director to a member of Congress, one of the most powerful Puerto Rican women in Massachusetts—reminds me that history does not dictate destiny. Fire meant to destroy can ignite resilience, and hatred meant to silence can be transformed into a voice that echoes for generations.

That is the irony and the triumph of my life; the same flames that sought to erase us became the fire that lit my path to power. Most importantly, it became the torch I now pass to the next generation. Mentoring young Puerto Rican and Latina women has been my way of ensuring that the barriers I broke are not rebuilt, that the power I claimed is multiplied, and that the legacy of resilience continues far beyond me.

ADVICE THAT CHANGED MY LIFE

One of the most powerful pieces of advice a mentor gave me was simple: "Never let anyone else define your worth." Those words became my anchor in spaces where my accent, gender, or heritage were treated as limitations. In politics, in education, and in life, I carried this truth with me. It reminded me that my identity was not a weakness, but a strength. Each time I faced discrimination, I repeated those words and turned doubt into determination. This advice shaped my confidence, grounded my leadership, and reminded me that my value comes from within— not from the labels others try to impose.

I learned early in my career about the importance of *"Keeping your word"* and would advise the reader that those three words will and can define you in your professional, and personal life as you move forward. Another piece of advice that is extremely important to me is, *"Service is love put into action."* It's not about recognition or power—rather it is how I feel about the responsibility of lifting others, creating opportunities, and opening doors where there are walls that are closed. My words, contribution and philosophy have been my journey and purpose beyond survival or personal success. Remember true leadership is not measured in titles, but in the progress we make. This advice became the guiding star of my life of service.

Biography

"When the door is closed because you're not wanted at the table, open it and take your seat! That is Gladys's philosophy.

Gladys's story reflects the rich and diverse heritage that has shaped her identity and worldview. As a Jibara from Cerro Gordo, San Lorenzo in Puerto Rico, she was raised with a deep connection to her roots, drawing strength from the Taino, African, and Spanish influences that have shaped her culture and community. The Jibara identity, often linked to rural Puerto Rican traditions, emphasizes self-reliance, resilience, and a strong sense of family.

Her family's move to South Boston, Massachusetts, during a time of social and racial turbulence added another layer to her personal narrative. The experiences of racism and discrimination that Gladys faced as part of the Puerto Rican diaspora in the United States would undoubtedly have had a profound impact on her worldview. These challenges likely instilled in her a strong sense of justice and a commitment to fighting for civil rights, human rights, and social equity.

In 1996 Gladys Rodriguez-Parker would make history when she was appointed District Director for United States Representative James P. McGovern (MA-03). In the history of the Massachusetts Congressional Delegation Gladys would be the first Puerto Rican woman to hold this post. Baptism by Fire! This position is responsible for overseeing the Congressman's

Massachusetts operations, facilitating communication between the district and the Washington office, coordinating with local elected officials, and providing constituent services.

As a trailblazer she would go on to open doors for other Latinos at the local, state and national levels. In addition to her official role Gladys dedicated her time on voter registration and education among Latino and marginalized communities. On election day she could be found bringing voters to the polls. This work required a great deal of civic education in neighborhoods where voters lived. Gladys has helped candidates for office up and down the ballot box at the local, state and national levels. Gladys was elected as a national delegate to represent the State of Massachusetts in presidential elections. She served as one of four Massachusetts Co-Chair for the Elect John Kerry for President campaign traveling around the country on his behalf.

Among the many groups, and organizations Gladys has been part of she is very proud of the Latino Education Institute (LEI) which she co-founded on the campus of Worcester State University. The LEI is dedicated to assist Latino students and their families with educational success. In addition to her work on getting a permanent home for the Puerto Rico 65th Infantry Borinqueneers a home on the Central MA Korean War Memorial in the City of Worcester.

Gladys became a single mother as a teenager, that did not deter her from graduating from high school and going on to the University of Massachusetts at Amherst and Worcester State

University. A Bachelor's and a Master's degree were obtained while balancing work and attending classes.

When Hurricane Maria devastated Puerto Rico, Gladys went to work calling upon people, helped to organize and create community events in support of those who left the island and found refuge in the City of Worcester. That work led to the creation of Amor Para Puerto Rico. As COVID-19 slammed the community, Gladys utilized her position and networks to assist in the fight against the pandemic.

Gladys Rodriguez-Parker

gladys.rodriguez1@gmail.com

BETWEEN TWO WORLDS: ROOTED IN LOVE, RISING THROUGH STRUGGLE

IRIS J. DELGADO

"You have to believe in yourself. You need to have the audacity to be great." ~ **Rosie Perez**

DEDICATION

In memory of my dearest mother Gloria Angelica Goden. Thank you for the privilege of being your daughter.

My story begins in the 1960s, in the warm countryside of Guayama, Puerto Rico. I grew up beside my grandmother, Mami. While my mother, Gloria, worked to support us, I was always by my grandmother's side—cooking over the fogón, washing clothes in the river, and sleeping beside her before the rooster's call. Being with her was the safest I ever felt. As a child, life felt humble, warm, and full of sweet memories.

My mother was fiercely protective and hardworking. Seeking a better future, she moved to New York City with courage, sacrifice, and hope, taking my youngest sister with her, and leaving my older sister and me temporarily with our grandmother. Not long after we joined her. It was the middle of winter, and I remember the magic of seeing snow for the first time—saving a cupful for my grandmother. But not long after, she passed away suddenly. I was too young to understand what I had lost. That lack of closure from not seeing her again left a deep wound I carried for years.

In New York City, our life was challenging, and the neighborhoods were dangerous and violent at times. My mother worked in factories, and I often served as her interpreter, navigating a system laced with racism and rejection. My resilience was born there—in the apartment windows where I watched the world unfold. Despite this, we found joy in little things—going to the park, beach, Sunday Mass, visiting friends, bargain shopping, watching telenovelas, and eating comfort food like rice and beans. I tried to adjust, but I missed my grandmother terribly and often felt emotionally lost.

Moving to Worcester, MA, in sixth grade offered a fresh start. For the first time, we could play outside. There were three-decker houses, nice parks, flowers, and downtown fun. I learned to ride a bike and roller skate, made my first best friend, excelled in school, was physically active, and encouraged. My sister and I loved to dance and learned the "Hustle" from visiting Nuyoricans. We went to the movies, helped in church, and spent summer days by the lake. These moments were healing.

Still, trauma lingered. In sixth grade, I was diagnosed with scoliosis. At 13, I had to wear a full-body brace, and by 14, I underwent a failed back surgery, leaving a broken metal rod in my back, a permanent limp, and chronic pain after thirty days in the hospital. I had a great team of adults helping me—especially my parents, teachers, and our church community. Though I could no longer run, I still found freedom in dancing once I was able to. My condition didn't define me, but it shaped how I moved through the world—with caution, pain, perseverance, and grit.

I learned independence from a young age—babysitting, selling candy, answering phones, and caring for the elderly—driven by fear of abandonment or not being "enough." A dreamer, masking sadness with humor and kindness, I found purpose in helping others while avoiding asking for help myself. Beneath the drive was a grieving child aching for a goodbye that never came, a silence whose impact I only understood decades later.

In my thirties, I attended a church retreat called "The Child Within" and had a breakthrough. I had lost one of my two mothers—my grandmother. That absence of goodbye became a lifelong ache. In that realization came peace and dialogue, leading me to speak more about it and finally move forward.

I was 47 when life tested me with a second failed spinal surgery, therapy, and limited mobility—but it never stole my spirit. I learned to adapt. Despite adversity, I grew into someone determined, creative, and deeply rooted in her Puerto Rican heritage. The challenges—physical, emotional, and cultural—shaped my resilience and empathy. I still carry pain from my loss and setbacks, but I "carry my cross" with dignity, guided by faith and gratitude.

I never ran again, but I danced. Though I struggled, I endured. My story, like many others who leave their island in search of something better, is one of love, loss, and the quiet, steady strength it takes to survive—and thrive—between two worlds. I didn't assimilate—I embraced the power of two identities. I became part of a new society personally and professionally while maintaining my Island roots, culture, and spirit of love as a proud Latina.

Our parents raised us in the Catholic faith, valued education, and encouraged hard work. Fluent in Spanish, some of us also learned to read and write it with our mother's help. Though college wasn't a topic much discussed at home, ambition led us to careers—mine in graphic design and librarianship, my siblings' in business, health, education, trades, criminal justice, administration, and the Marine Corps.

When I first sat with my North High School guidance counselor in 1981 to find a summer job, the last thing on my mind was that one day I would become the first Latina Professional Public Librarian in Worcester which required a master's degree in library and information science—in the second most populous city in the state, serving over 210,000 people. The counselor kindly told me about an open position as a clerk-typist at the Worcester Public Library. I had just earned a clerk-typist certificate, so I said I'd "take it for now." I usually went to the library just to study because it was hard for me to concentrate at home. Back then, the library seemed quiet, dreary, and far from the creative world I loved.

My true passion was the arts—chorus, dance, drama, guitar, sewing, woodworking, design—but above all, drawing. Drawing gave me a sense of power, belonging, and identity. I was ambitious and curious, but also introverted and shy. Life had already taught me loss and resilience, so over time I learned I could be both introvert and extrovert—an ambivert—depending on the moment.

The year I graduated high school, I thought I'd be starting art school. Instead, at 18, I began working full time at the library, got married, left home, and became a proud mother to my son, Luis, and later to my daughter, Dyjani. My marriage lasted 13 years, and my career at the library lasted 41—years of opportunities, learning, and growth.

Ironically, I wasn't even hired after being interviewed. I was called back a week later only because the woman who was hired had been let go. That unexpected second chance opened the door to six promotions over my library career. A couple of years in, I upgraded to secretary, then in 1985 appointed as a neighborhood Children's Librarian.

One of the most influential people in my journey was my lifetime mentor, Christine Kardokas, Head of Reference and later Assistant Library Director. Christine had an extraordinary gift for spotting potential in others. She pushed me toward opportunities I never imagined for myself— introducing me to leaders in spaces like City Hall, and planting the seed that would grow into my decision to attend college at 31. She believed in me when I was still learning to believe in myself. Christine never pulled the ladder up—she steadied it so I could climb. That lesson became the heartbeat of my work as a librarian.

At the Main South Branch Library, I immersed myself in a vibrant, multilingual community, building relationships with families, schools, and organizations. My colleague, Robert Caldwell, Head of the Branch Library, taught me that leadership is as much about encouragement as it is about expertise. His joy and energy reminded me daily that when you uplift others, you rise together.

In the late 1980s, I joined the "Latino Leaders of the Future" program hosted by United Way. It opened my eyes to the power of civic engagement and inspired me to serve on local organizational boards—an early step into the broader world of leadership.

In 1990, funding cuts forced most branch libraries to close, and I returned to the Main Library, dividing my time between the bookmobile and the Great Brook Valley Neighborhood Branch Library (GBV), a hub for the city's growing Spanish-speaking population. There, my bilingual skills became a bridge—helping families navigate resources, offering children a place where their language was not a barrier but a gift.

Not everyone saw it that way. I still remember a library worker asking why I spoke Spanish "if I lived in America." That only fueled my belief that bilingualism was a treasure to be protected and celebrated. Even when I faced prejudice—or jealousy from those who noticed patrons gravitating toward me as a Latina—I met it with professionalism, not defensiveness; power with grace.

While at GBV, I took a chance and asked for a promotion. I earned it and became the first Head Librarian of the GBV Branch Library. That experience cemented my belief that true leadership isn't about pushing others aside—it's about lifting others as you rise.

Driven by my passion for creativity, I pursued an associate's degree in computer graphic design and illustration from Quinsigamond Community College in 1997, then a bachelor's degree in communications with a concentration in graphic design from Fitchburg State University. My artistic skills found a home in the library's marketing and promotions, blending my love for design with my commitment to community.

2001 was my chance to advance once again, I began a graduate level Children's Librarian position at the Main Library. Christine urged me to take the next leap—earning my master's in library and information science. I hesitated. Could I handle the workload? Was I capable? A colleague warned me libraries were becoming obsolete in the digital age. She was wrong. I realized the only thing holding me back was fear. I pushed through and decided I would now be taking a seat at the front of the class. Twelve years of part-time college classes later, I walked across Simmons College stage in 2006, degree in hand—finally a "true professional" librarian in title, as well as spirit.

From there, I embraced every opportunity—attending conferences, joining library organizations, including REFORMA National, meeting Latina librarians who showed me representation mattered, and designing culturally rich programs that made families feel at home. My outreach extended to teen moms, migrants, homeless shelters, schools, and community centers. I wanted Latinos in Worcester to see the library as their space, a place they belonged.

When a youth management position opened, my colleagues encouraged me to apply, seeing strengths I still doubted in myself. I asked, Why me? The answer was simple: Because I was ready.

As Youth Services Manager, I led with gratitude— determined to make our department the best in the state, a place where children, teens, and families felt welcome, inspired, and empowered. For eight years, I took pride in leading a team, to make our spaces warm and inviting, and to create programs that sparked curiosity and joy. When people asked me for the person in charge, I'd smile and say, "That's me." Along the way, I proved something to those who doubted me—and maybe even to myself: Leadership is not a title, it's a responsibility.

I never stopped learning, growing, and lifting others—just as Christine taught me all those years ago. By 2015, Christine had passed away, and I know she would have been proud.

This is not a story of defeat—it is a story of rising. From the campo of Puerto Rico to the boroughs of New York, to the neighborhoods of Worcester, I endured, adapted, and blossomed. My strength is rooted in love. My survival is a quiet triumph. My story is proof that even when we come from humble beginnings, face heartbreaking loss, and carry visible and invisible scars—we are not broken; we will rise.

Looking back, my career was never about books or buildings—it was about people. It was about believing in someone's potential before they believe it themselves. It was about creating spaces where others could dream bigger, reach higher, and walk-through doors that might otherwise have been closed.

Because "great leaders don't close the door behind them"— they hold it open, they invite others in, and they make sure the room is big enough for everyone.

ADVICE THAT CHANGED MY LIFE

My mentor once told me, "Some people are educated, but they're not always smart." Then she added, "Iris, you are smart—even without finishing college—because you seize opportunities that others with degrees often let pass." I realized that being "smart" meant paying attention, being resourceful, and not letting fear or hesitation hold me back. It's about awareness, courage, and action. Credentials are important, but they do not replace action, vision, or heart. I carry that lesson with me every day. Whenever doubt creeps in, I remind myself to step forward with confidence and embrace opportunities instead of hesitating.

A phrase that has guided and empowered me for years is: "To get something you never had, you have to do something you never did." The unknown will always feel intimidating until you give yourself the chance to try. Whether it's a new opportunity, experience, or challenge, you'll never know what it can bring unless you take that first step. Trying something and later deciding it's not for you doesn't mean failure—it means growth. Each attempt adds to your strength and wisdom, opening doors you might never have seen if you hadn't dared to move forward.

Biography

Iris Delgado was born in Puerto Rico and later lived in New York City before moving with her parents and seven siblings to Worcester, MA, in the late 1970s. At 31, while married with two children, she returned to school, earning an associate degree in graphic design from Quinsigamond Community College, a bachelor's in communications from Fitchburg State, and a master's in library and information science from Simmons College.

Starting at the Worcester Public Library at 18, Iris rose from clerk to children's librarian, branch head, and eventually manager of the state's second-largest children's department. In 2006, she became Worcester's first Latina Professional Public Librarian.

She expanded services for the Latino/Hispanic community through bilingual storytimes, cultural celebrations, and outreach to families, schools, shelters, and migrants. Known for her expertise in children's literature, she shaped programs for diverse families in a rapidly changing city.

Iris retired in 2023 after 41 years of service. She now works in marketing for Literacy Volunteers of Greater Worcester. As President of Adelante Worcester, the HACE Committee, the Latino History Project of Worcester, and leader in cultural and educational initiatives, she's earned, among others, the YWCA Erskine Award, WLDS Visions Award, and an ALX100 nomination.

Iris J Delgado

cotto66.ic@gmail.com

VOICES RISING

JASMIN RIVAS

"I will participate in changing the situation of injustice and inequality that I encounter because they deny people their right and destroy their potential." -
Dr. Antonia Pantoja, Puerto Rican educator, feminist, civil rights leader, and founder of ASPIRA

DEDICATION

To my sons, their children and all who read my story long after I am gone; may you find courage, joy and love within these pages and within yourselves.

Poderosa,

Like Mama Chu, wise and beautiful.

Who woke up every day to feed chickens and tend the garden at age one hundred.

I noticed as a child, I had the same hands.

Hands for helping.

Hands for healing.

I raised one of those hands when I was sworn in as a town councilor in June 2022, the second Latina to ever do so in Southbridge, Massachusetts. I served my community proudly for those three years, tending to the garden of people that call the town home.

I stood side by side with high school students as they protested the injustices of a state receivership. I coordinated a community forum so their voices would be heard. A good leader creates space for multiple perspectives.

I am protective of my community. Their struggles mirror mine. The demanding work to make ends meet, the subtle and not so subtle racism, I still walk in those shoes sometimes. The times when I have been laughed at and silenced by men in power. The times my ideas have been disregarded and then adopted when they came from a colonizer's voice. Those are the times I think about my ancestors on the island, the obstacles they overcame and how resilient they were. They give me strength to keep fighting for what is right.

Poderosa,

Like Abuela Candita,

Storyteller,

I learned so many lessons listening at the foot of her bed.

I don't look like Abuela Candita, who had milky light skin, a regal aura and petite stature, but I am tough like her. We both overcame domestic violence.

Like abuela, I took on multiple jobs to make ends meet and not have to depend on an abusive partner. We followed our instincts, even when people told us it was better to stay and not make waves.

I escaped the abuse of my oldest son's father when I left everything I knew in Southbridge and moved to Nashville, Tennessee back in 1994. I had been saving money from working at Zawada Insurance in Worcester, hiding it in my shoes so he would not find it. I was just waiting for the right time.

The abuse did not start right away. It gradually shifted from his controlling behavior and verbal insults when I was pregnant to something much more physical after I had the baby. I tried to fight back but he was quick on his feet and so much stronger than me. The final straw was when he put his hands on our baby boy. I would not allow him to abuse Adonis.

My parents and I devised a plan. My brother helped. I waited until he was on one of his all-day excursions at his homies house to drink, smoke and hang out. I did not have to give notice to the insurance agency because he had made me quit after one of his jealous rages. I packed a bag for me and the baby, put him in his carrier, grabbed my money, and fled out of the apartment we had rented together.

My parents, who were waiting outside, drove me to (my brother) Frank's apartment. I had bought a one-way ticket the week before. My friend would pick us up. I could stay at her place. She was also a survivor of abuse. She knew what I was going through.

I was anxious that night. I thought for sure my son's father would find me and beat me until I went back home with him. The next morning, Frank dropped us off at Worcester Airport. I boarded the tiny plane to safety and freedom.

I want more women and girls to have that same confidence to know when they need to go. I try to be a role model to the young women in my family. I want them to learn from my mistakes. My stories are a way to share my newfound wisdom with future generations.

Poderosa,
Like Abuela Juana,
Caretaker,
Grounded,
Mother Earth,

Braver than all the men as she stomped out the tarantula under my feet when I was twelve-years-old sitting at the kitchen table en la casita de mis abuelos en Juncos, Puerto Rico.

As I get older, I look more like Abuela Juana. My wiry salt and pepper hair and pear-shaped body resemble my Afro-Indigenous abuela from the small, mountain town. As a child, I wasn't always proud of what I looked like. The boys at school talked about how "different" I looked. It never sounded like a compliment. It made me self-conscious. I would try to play it off like it didn't bother me, but I wondered why I couldn't look like the other girls in my class and in the books I read. My dolls all had straight hair. Nancy Drew and the Hardy boys all had straight hair. That's why I would never complain when my mom ironed my hair on the ironing board. I thought if I fit in more the bullying would stop. It never did.

It was not until fifth grade when I saw Puerto Rican families from Southbridge in a book my teacher wrote that I realized stories about people like me were out there. It made me feel more confident. It helped me not care so much about the boys picking on me.

Before that I only knew folk tales about our people, like the one about the Taina Princess and the Spanish soldier. I learned them from my mom. It was hard to distinguish if they had been real people or just made-up characters. My teacher's book was about real people living in Southbridge. These were families my family knew. It made me feel so empowered. Our stories were important.

I later learned much more of our history I was never taught in school, like the stories of the Independistas, writers and advocates on the island. These were people that fought the colonization of Puerto Rico. They wrote about our struggles and resilience. They were people who loved the island so much they would give their lives for it.

I felt so much pride in being Boricua. I came to appreciate all the various parts of who I am. Now, I embrace and show off my curly hair. I also fight for inclusive curriculum so that generations of Latinos after me don't have to wait to see themselves in the books they read.

Poderosa,
Like my mother,
A survivor,
Resilient.

My mother (Daisy) used to be a librarian in Puerto Rico. She wrote stories and poetry when she was younger. I get my passion for reading and writing from her. It must be why I felt drawn to books in elementary school. I became a library aid in middle school and later when I became a mom myself, I volunteered for (my younger son) Evan's school library.

Books were my escape as a kid. I could travel to different worlds and pretend I was a rich princess from a foreign land. I did not have to think about having to use paper food stamps to buy milk at the corner store. I could act like I didn't care that my family could not afford the dance lessons at Debbie Sichol's Dance School.

As I got older, I started writing my own stories. In middle school, I wrote a fictional story about a unicorn. In high school, my writing got deeper. I wrote poetry about my life growing up as a Puerto Rican girl in a small New England town. I wrote about boys who broke my heart and the lessons that taught me. I also wrote for the yearbook club. I was tasked with creating copy that made the theme come to life. I loved weaving the words together to paint a picture for the reader.

When I left home to go to Michigan State University, I chose to pursue a career in journalism. Finding the truth and telling the story was what called to me. As the first person in my family to go to college, I dreamed of adventure. I could be a foreign correspondent in the middle of a war, getting to the truth of what was happening. I could be a sports reporter, interviewing Larry Bird on the court after a game. I could be a news anchor. I could become the Puerto Rican Connie Chung! The possibilities seemed endless.

Poderosa,
Like my sisters,
Brenda, wise beyond her years, a doctorate in her pocket.
Jannette, a force to be reckoned with.

The middle is where you blend in, but it can also be where you stand out. I am one of the four children my mother gave birth to. Jannette is the oldest, followed by Frank, me, and Brenda, "la bebé" as my mom calls her. Jannette and Frank are children born from my mom's first marriage. Her first husband wasn't great. My mom calls him a "sinvergüenza". So, my dad (Jose, most people call him Cheo) raised them since they were kids. They are like 8-10 years older than me.

When I was five years old and we lived in Hartford Connecticut, Jannette and Frank were teenagers. They played instruments in the school band and competed in salsa dance competitions. I worshipped the ground they walked on. They did not feel that way about me.

I remember how Jannette would make me walk behind her and her boyfriend when we were sent to the store by my mom. She called me a "little pest." I was not fazed. She didn't know it then, but Jannette helped me learn to be more independent. I also learned to be fast to keep up with her.

Frank had the best record collection. I loved listening to the Motown beats from the room I shared with Jannette down the hall. I would practice the hustle dance moves I saw them perform together. Sometimes, when Frank wasn't home, I would sneak into his room and borrow his records to play on my toy record player. I would put them back in his collection before he got home. It didn't matter how careful I was he always knew when I had been in his room. He would get so mad and yell at me. I would go crying to my mom. Mom would yell at him. She would then scold me. Nobody won. It never stopped me. I just learned to be more resourceful.

I never understood what the big deal was until Brenda was born. She looked like one of my dolls with those cute, chubby cheeks. Finally, I would have someone to play with me. We would sit together in my cardboard house in our apartment on Mechanic Street in Southbridge to have café with our dolls.

Unfortunately for Brenda, when I became a hormonal teenager, I couldn't stand her. I pushed her away just like my older siblings had done to me. I was cruel and played tricks on her with my cousins. My mom would yell at me and try to throw la chancleta.

As an adult, I appreciate my siblings, the lessons they taught me and the relationships that grew out of those challenges. My sons grew up around my siblings and my parents who helped me raise them to be the kindhearted young men they are today. My village was there for me when I needed them the most. It's something I hope my sons remember when they have families of their own. No matter what you have been through, no matter how far you may be, family should be there for each other.

Poderosa,
Mind, Body, Soul.
Ancestors speak through me,
Han Han Katu.

Mother,

Writer,

Healer,

My purpose says, lift their voices.

I stand up and shout,

Poderosa!

ADVICE THAT CHANGED MY LIFE

The best piece of advice that I still remember today came from my friend Wanda Viruet, who passed away in 2021. I remember Wanda telling me to always hold my head high and sit up straight like the intelligent and powerful Latina woman that I was. She told me never to shy away from who I was meant to be. She always saw the light in me even when I couldn't. She knew I could do so much more to help our community. That's why she encouraged me to run for Town Council. I wasn't sure I could win. She believed in me and helped me believe in myself. She was such an inspiration.

I never got a chance to tell her that I was running. She never got a chance to see me win. I know her spirit was with me though. I still hear her encouraging me. I will never forget her and what a strong Latina she was. I always looked up to her. Her laugh and her energy could always light up a room. She did so much for our community. She was my mentor.

Biography

Jasmin Rivas is a Puerto Rican woman, mother, poet, community activist, educator, and the President of Jaz- Yoga/ Health and Wellness living in Southbridge. She works to empower youth as the Program Director for the Coalition for Anti-Racism and Equity Inc. (CARE). Previously, Jasmin broke new ground as the first Director of Diversity, Equity, Inclusion, and Access at Old Sturbridge Village. Her determination helped her become only the second Latina elected to the Southbridge Town Council, where she advocated for the most vulnerable in her community for three years.

In 2020, Jasmin co-wrote two collaborative poems published in Bay Path University's *Multiplicity Magazine.* In 2012, she received an *Elite 13' Writers Award* from Chapter 13' Poet Society. She has been a featured poet at events in Worcester and Southbridge. Jasmin also worked as a reporter and editor at the Southbridge Evening News.

Jasmin holds a BA in English from Worcester State University, an MFA in Creative Writing from Bay Path University, a Diversity, Equity, and Inclusion Certificate from Cornell University, and a 200-hour yoga certification through Breathe For Change (Yoga Alliance member). She is also pursuing a Breathe For Change MEd in Social Emotional Learning, Mindfulness, and Yoga at Woolf University, Europe.

Jasmin Rivas

Jasminrivas555@yahoo.com

Facebook: Jasmin Rivas

Facebook: Jaz-Yoga/Health and Wellness

Instagram: jriv555

LinkedIn: Jasmin Riv

OPENING DOORS: A JOURNEY OF LOVE,
RESILIENCE, AND PURPOSE

JEANET LADINO-OTERO

"The question isn't who is going to let me; it's who is going to stop me." — **Ayn Rand**

DEDICATION

To my mother and grandmother in heaven, whose eternal love lights my way.

To my Aunt Ellie, and Tuti, and my cousins, for grounding me in wisdom, faith, and family.

To my husband Vic, my stepchildren, and my dogs, for reminding me that love is life's purest joy.

And to all who've guided me—your faith in me fuels my purpose, grace, and gratitude with every step I take.

My name is Jeanet, and I am originally from Colombia. My journey has been shaped not only by the places I've been and the roles I've held, but by the people who have walked alongside me, the love that grounded me, and the unwavering belief that we are meant to lift each other as we climb. This is a story about perseverance, grace, and the quiet power of community.

ROOTS

I grew up in Colombia, where I attended a catholic school that shaped the foundation of my values. The lessons I learned there—discipline, humility, compassion, and faith—became the compass that continues to guide me. But more than any institution, my greatest teachers were the women who raised me. My mother, my aunt Ellie, and my grandmother were the pillars of my childhood. Each of them carried strength wrapped in tenderness. They showed me how to hold my head high, work with purpose, and lead with heart. They were not just caregivers; they were builders of spirit and soul. The love they gave, the sacrifices they made, and the example they set became the blueprint for who I strive to be each day.

Throughout my upbringing, I was blessed to encounter teachers who saw something in me, something I hadn't yet recognized in myself. One of those early mentors was my systems teacher, Wenceslao. He not only taught me in the classroom but also helped open the door to my first professional opportunity at a very important financial institution in Colombia.

Still, I've learned that doors don't open just because we hope they will. They open when we are brave enough to knock, when we show up, build trust, and speak our truth. That courage, that self-belief, is something I learned slowly, and sometimes painfully, over the course of my life.

A NEW COUNTRY, A NEW BEGINNING

In 1992, I came to the United States with hope in my heart and uncertainty in my hands. The transition wasn't easy. Like many immigrants, I had to start over. My career paused. My confidence wavered. But I never stopped trying.

I found work in the hospitality industry, in a hotel far from the path I had once imagined. Yet, that experience gave me something profound—an understanding of people, of kindness, of service. Those early customer service skills became a cornerstone of how I lead today. I learned that no matter where you begin, every job has value, every experience teaches, and every person deserves dignity.

Later, I accepted a job in accounting, far from my passion, and not where I felt most equipped. But when you are building a new life in a new land, you don't always get to choose what's next. You take the opportunities offered, and you give them your best. You keep showing up until the next door appears.

Eventually, I found my way back to education. I returned to school and completed my master's degree. That choice wasn't easy; it required long nights, sacrifices, and moments of doubt. But investing in myself was one of the most powerful decisions I've made. Education reminded me of who I was. It reconnected me with my voice and gave me new tools to build the future I dreamed of.

During that time, I met a beautiful group of friends who shared that dream. Together, we tried to build an e-commerce business. It wasn't a financial success, but it was a deeply meaningful chapter. We supported one another, mentored one another, and learned together. That endeavor, though short-lived, was another kind of door; one that opened our minds and hearts.

FINDING MY PLACE AT A PRESTIGIOUS FINANCIAL INSTITUTION

Not long after completing my degree, I joined a prestigious financial institution. That decision marked the beginning of a life-changing journey. I started as an officer. At first, I still saw myself through the lens of "follower," someone who needed permission, someone who waited to be told. But that changed after a single conversation.

One day, my manager said, "You're a professional. You don't have to ask permission. Tell me what you need, and how you'll manage it." That sentence was more than a workplace policy; it was a gift. It gave me permission to see myself differently, to lead.

From there, I was given more responsibilities, projects, team management, and reporting. For the first time I began to feel I truly belonged in leadership. It wasn't just about managing work it was about shaping direction, inspiring others, and making an impact.

Within the institution, I transitioned across several roles, expanding my expertise into cybersecurity and risk management. These weren't paths I had originally envisioned, but each gave me a new perspective and deeper purpose. Again, it wasn't just about the roles, it was about the people who believed in me. Each time someone gave me a chance, they passed me a torch I now feel honored to carry for others.

BECOMING A DOOR-OPENER

The most transformative shift in my career happened when I joined an employee network. Until then, my story had been shaped by those who opened doors for me. But through this network, I began opening doors for others. As Chair, I witnessed how many, especially early-career employees, struggled to find access to mentorship and opportunity. So, we built something. We launched a mentorship program particularly designed for them, to empower, uplift, and prepare colleagues for advancement.

The results were remarkable. That first year, our team received a national award. The following year, we were recognized again as one of the best employee networks. But beyond accolades, what mattered most was the change I saw in people's eyes. The light that flickered on when they felt seen, heard, and supported.

Since then, I've had the privilege of mentoring over 75 individuals. I don't just help them polish resumes or prepare for interviews. I help them recognize that their skills are transferable, their stories matter, and that they belong in rooms they once thought were closed to them.

Today, I am a Vice President at a prestigious financial institution, leading a team of seven. I don't take that lightly. Every day, I wake up grateful, not only for the work I do, but for the people I serve. My leadership is grounded in empathy. I don't believe in barking orders or standing on titles. I believe in collaboration, encouragement, and creating space for others to speak. I remember what it felt like to question whether I belonged. And now, I do everything I can to ensure my team knows they do. I lead with kindness, because I know it works. I lead with purpose, because I know it's contagious. And I lead with humility, because every role no matter how "small" it may seem is a steppingstone to something greater.

A LIFE FULL OF MEANING

My story isn't just about career progression. It's about love. About community. About resilience. It's about starting over, falling down, and getting up again. It's about my roots in Colombia, where women taught me what real strength looks like.

It's about the teachers and mentors who saw me before I saw myself. It's about colleagues and friends who grew alongside me. And now, it's about being the person who says to others, "You can do this. I believe in you."

Through it all, the greatest blessing in my life has been my family. My husband—my best friend and steadfast cheerleader—has always believed in me, even in the moments I doubted myself. His quiet strength lifts me, and his love sustains me. My children and our dogs are the heartbeat of my world, grounding me with unconditional love and laughter. They are my sanctuary, my joy, and the reason I keep moving forward with purpose and hope.

As I reflect on this journey, I am reminded that every success is built on the shoulders of those who came before us, and the hands of those who walk beside us. I want my story to be a reminder that even when the path isn't clear, you can carve it. That even when doors don't open on their own, you can knock loudly and bravely. And when you have the opportunity to open a door for someone else, you must.

We are all here because someone believed in us. And the most beautiful legacy we can leave is to believe in someone else.

ADVICE THAT CHANGED MY LIFE

As I reflect on this journey, I am reminded that every success is built on the shoulders of those who came before us, and the hands of those who walk beside us.

I want my story to be a reminder that even when the path isn't clear, you can carve it. That even when doors don't open on their own, you can knock loudly and bravely. And when you have the opportunity to open a door for someone else, you must.

Because we are all here because someone believed in us. My key message is simple: leadership is not about titles, but about impact, courage, and lifting others forward. The most beautiful legacy we can leave is to believe in someone else.

Biography

Jeanet Ladino-Otero, originally from Colombia, moved to the United States in 1992. She is a passionate advocate for mentorship, inclusion, and community empowerment. Jeanet led the creation of the Hispanic and Latin Cambridge College Alumni Association and currently serves as President of the United Latinas Massachusetts Chapter, where she supports women and promotes Latino-owned businesses.

She served as Global Co-Chair of the Professional Women's Network (PWN) and Chair of the Latin American Professionals Network (LAPN), where she developed impactful programs for employee engagement. Under her leadership, LAPN earned the Top 25 Diversity Impact Award and was named Top Employee Network for the Latina 50 Style.

Jeanet earned her master's degree in management, information security, and e-commerce from Cambridge College in Boston. She is a Five-Star Pacesetter for the Jimmy Fund Foundation, walking the Boston Marathon route annually to raise funds. She also organizes a toy drive for children in Bogotá through the Civic Police.

She lives near Boston with her husband Vic, and is a stepmom to four boys and mom to three dogs. Jeanet is deeply committed to mentoring women of color and creating spaces for growth and leadership.

Jeanet is currently Vice President in HR Risk Oversight, Controls & Advisory for a financial institution in Boston.

Jeanet Ladino-Otero

ladino.otero.jeanet@gmail.com

A MOTHER'S LOVE

JESSIKA ROZKI

"Your passion will lead you to your purpose!"

DEDICATION

To my madre, gracias por enseñarme a ser una madre luchadora y siempre presente.

To my boys, Omar, Romelo, and Joaxis, thank you for loving me through every season, through struggles, triumphs, and all my business dreams. You are my peace and strength.

To my daughter Zahra, I thank God for choosing me to be your mother and giving me the best friend I needed.

To my future grandbabies, Mima broke generational curses so you live in faith, gratitude, love, and purpose.

May the Lord guide every reader to their purpose.

From a high school dropout to a teenage mom, battling with domestic violence, depression, anxiety, and low-self-esteem to finding my purpose. My children showed me unconditional love, and they survived with me—the good, the bad and the ugly—but most importantly they saw how I overcame every obstacle to become the mother they deserved, the woman God intended me to be. As you read my story, I pray that you will find your purpose and become the greatest version of you.

I was seven years old when my mother and I stepped off the plane into a cold September sky. The steamy warmth I'd always known in Puerto Rico was gone, replaced by crisp air that took my breath away. I grabbed my mother's hand as we joined a small line of travelers at the airport—my heart pounding, my skin tingling at the unfamiliar chill. Ahead lay Massachusetts—a strange land, full of promise and uncertainty. A new city, a new world.

I remember so vividly her tears when we were left behind in an empty apartment to fend for ourselves. Her language barrier made it even more difficult to find work, but we never lacked food or a safe place to sleep, clothes on our backs and shoes on our feet. Many nights I saw her tears roll down her cheeks and I could feel her sadness and worries.

As a teenager I didn't have any guidance nor people who could speak life into me. All I knew was that I wanted more out of life and I had to work hard, so I decided to drop out of high school and became a manager at a fast food chain company.

When I became a mother for the first time in 1999, I felt love like no other. He looked so perfect with soft baby skin and the most beautiful brown eyes. Was this the kind of love my mom felt for my siblings and me? An unconditional love so pure and magical. Life looked so different, and I couldn't help but think about life in a whole new way. I decided to enroll in a teenage mothers' program to get my GED. That's where I met a teacher that changed my outlook on life. "You can be anything you want to be," were the words that have stuck with me until this day. He believed in me!

Now a mother of two amazing boys, I was working endless jobs with no future at hand. I decided to become a school bus driver to be able to have a good paying job, provide for my boys, and create a better future for us. I loved every minute of it. My boss was such an amazing man. He helped me keep my job after going through one of the hardest times of my life, which I lived in silence—a life of domestic violence from a man who I had loved for most of the young years of my life. Pregnant once again with my third child, I kept asking myself, *God, how can this be? He was my best friend. How can he love me and cause me so much heartache at the same time? Lord, I can't keep going through this. I deserve better. My children deserve better, but here I am trying to fix what's already broken.* My heart sank as I swallowed every tear looking at the blackeye from a man I was so deeply in love with. I called out of work due to fear of losing my job. A week later, I returned wearing sunglasses to hide my eye. A close friend, noticing my reluctance to meet her gaze, gently took my hand as tears ran down my face. I felt so ashamed, "How can a woman like me, with so much love to give, allow a man to put their hands on me?" I had no words, and she hugged me so tight, endlessly.

For many years I battled the feeling of abandonment, low self-esteem, depression, and anxiety, caused by the absence of my father. It's been so many years wondering why he never looked for me. What did I do wrong? Why doesn't he call me or at least check up on me? I still don't have those answers, and maybe I never will but what matters to me is ensuring my children never feel as I once did. My love for transporting children to and from school helped me to navigate all those challenges. Knowing that a simple, "Good morning," could change a child's life. I worked tirelessly and started seeing places and homes I could never imagine. For the first time, I saw beautiful homes in other neighborhoods and wondered what their owners did for a living so I might achieve similar success one day. I thought those were only things that rich people on TV could have, not a girl like me.

God found me broken but I never lost hope. I cried for many nights asking him to take away all this pain, this heartache which made me feel like I was slowly dying. Days turned into weeks, until one day I said, "God show me that you are real. I do not want to live like this. Help me, I can't do this on my own. I need you. My boys need you. Help me raise them." I heard music from my window playing inside the church across the street. The melody was like no other. I walked across the street and surrendered it all to God. It was one of the hardest and most courageous things I have ever done. Months later, I joined a small group of women who poured so much love into me, helped me heal, taught me how to understand the word of God, and how to pray. I felt whole for the very first time in my life. I fell in love with what God did within me, and I decided to open my home to start my own woman's Bible study group and help women from every walk of life. I felt full of life with so much joy, and I wanted to share that feeling with so many other women. That was when my life began. I was a new creation in Christ and met my second husband.

Motherhood found me once again with more wisdom and a deeper sense of self. This time, it wasn't about starting over, it was about rising higher on my own terms. This child arrived not to complete me but to walk beside the woman I was becoming. This time it was so different. It was a beautiful baby girl, and I wanted to be a stay-at-home mom, but soon after postpartum depression hit home. I asked myself, *Lord, am I a bad mother because I felt sad and blue?* I slowly started to realize that I missed working as a bus driver and being a mother, so I prayed and asked God, "Lord, give me a vision, so I can help other parents with the skills that I have while I raise my daughter." God revealed it to me in my dream and showed me exactly the vehicle and my daughter in it with other children. Within a year or less Rozki Rides was born.

For several months I researched day in and day out: How to be a legal uber driver for kids? The craziest part was that

I didn't even know how to use a computer, but that didn't stop me. I kept on researching, asking questions every chance I got. I joined many free entrepreneur programs and met so many people. At one of the events they had I met someone who I shared my business idea with, and he brushed me off. I felt so disrespected, but it gave me even more power to keep pursuing my dream, my goals and my purpose.

After purchasing my first minivan in 2019, I launched Rozki Rides Transportation while learning how to balance family life. The more I pursued it, the more my second marriage crumbled. He was not happy with the idea of me working again, but failed to realize that I was drowning in my sorrow. My postpartum depression was more than I could bear, and this new idea was helping me in more ways than I could imagine.

Many times, it was exhausting, and I wanted to quit. I cried so much, especially when I didn't understand why my husband couldn't understand my vision. No one understood me and the hardest part was feeling so alone. The support I was expecting from my family and friends was not what I was expecting. They kept telling me I was obsessing. The people who I cared for most were nowhere to be found. I was once again feeling alone and abandoned, but this time I was stronger and wiser. I had God on my side. "He never leaves us nor forsakes us" (Hebrew 13:5).

I learn differently than others and it takes me longer to process information, but when I get it, I get it. Back when I was pregnant with my second son, I met one of the most amazing teachers and one of his best pieces of advice to me was, "You can be anything you want to be. Books have everything you need." I never took that for granted. I just knew I was different and being different is actually a great thing.

Rozki Rides, safe, reliable, and professional transportation company specializing in student transportation services and under-served communities. Rozki Rides was built with a mission and passion to provide quality services and exceptional customer care creating a different dynamic in children's transportation. Many saw it as just another transportation company but to me it was a ministry. I have many drivers who believe in God as much as I do, and share the gospel with our students, respectfully. As the owner I pray over my vehicles, employees, and all the children we transport, including my daughter. Something that started as a hobby became one of the most trusted transportation companies in Western Massachusetts. In the last few years, we purchased brand new 2025 buses and 2025 vans and added more staff. I have had the privilege of serving as a keynote speaker for audiences of over 400 people in different conferences focused on leadership and innovation, to mentor many women and become a leader to my children and the people around me.

My oldest son became a teacher, wrestling coach, and an amazing brother. My middle son runs the company alongside me and is also a wrestling coach. My youngest son plans on becoming an entrepreneur (he loves to cook) and will be graduating soon. As for my daughter, she is currently in school, and I get to bring her there daily. I am one of the proudest mothers in the world.

A mother's love empowers us to overcome challenges we never anticipated. My faith gives me purpose and strength through hardship, showing me unconditional support. For my children, I am committed to breaking generational curses and striving for greatness. Though I sometimes question my worth, I remember who I belong to and give thanks for my growth and the journey ahead.

ADVICE THAT CHANGED MY LIFE

Once someone said to me "Create the life you want to live" from that day on I decided to work hard, stay focused and create a life worth living. Life is what you make of it. Live it and Live it well.

Biography

Jessika Rozki is a proud mom of four with more than 19 years of experience in the transportation industry, a certified 7D trainer and CDL School Bus Driver Instructor. The founder of Rozki Rides, LLC, a growing transportation company based in Springfield, Massachusetts, known for its safe, family-friendly, and community-focused service. What started as a local solution for busy families has grown into a trusted brand under Jessika's leadership, vision, and relentless drive.

Balancing motherhood and entrepreneurship, Jessika has built a business that reflects her values—reliability, care, and connection. Her inspiring journey has made her a sought-after voice in business and leadership spaces. She's been a keynote speaker at the Women's Conference in Springfield, the BECMA Conference in Boston, and this November will take the stage as the keynote speaker at the Super 60 Conference just to name a few.

Jessika is passionate about empowering women, especially moms, to believe in their ideas and take bold steps toward success. Whether she's leading her team, driving change in her community, or sharing her story on stage, she leads with heart, purpose, and hustle.

Jessika Rozki

jessika@rozkirides.com

www.rozkirides.com

Facebook: Rozkirides

Instagram: @RozkiRides

WHO AM I? I AM PODEROSA

KARYN R. SANCHEZ

"It does not matter how slowly you go as long as you do not stop." - **Confucius**

DEDICATION

To my spouse and kids for all their support throughout this process and inspiring me to move forward with this writing venture. To my parents for showing me how to believe in myself.

To my grandfather who passed away this August, thank you for always being there;

Thank you for showing me there's a lot of life to live and the importance of having goals and aspirations and to go after them.

Have you been living your life by the identity given to you by others? For more than two-thirds of my life, that is how I was living. However, over the last 10 years, I have been consciously working on redefining myself, shaping the identity I want, and as a result, I embarked on a journey that I never would have imagined.

LETTING GO OF LIMITING BELIEFS

I remember struggling many times throughout my career when I noticed time and again how disparate treatment towards women created an unfair playing field. Perhaps what really irked me was that it was not obvious to everyone that the starting line for women was at least 50 yards back, if not more. So many times, I have been tempted to give up. Whether it was because of my race, my nationality, my skin color, my hair type, my ethnicity, my age, my culture, my gender, I realized there will always be something that would try to hold me back, and that I am not the only one facing struggles. So, I decided to try to let go of limiting beliefs and really lean into my strengths!

Throughout most of my education, I always found myself needing to prove my capabilities. During my adolescence, we lived in a town that at the time was not diverse. There was a handful of minorities, and I always felt as if I didn't belong. I took all honors classes and AP classes, but at the beginning of each school year, I always felt as if the teachers thought I did not belong or I was just there to fill a quota.

Then, in my first year of undergraduate studies, I was taking a course that second-year students take, but I met the prerequisite, so I was able to enroll. During the first week, the professor pulled me aside one day and told me that normally the class is only taken by older students, and the level of the class is a bit high. She thought that because I was a first-year student that I might find the class too difficult and that I might want to consider dropping the class before the drop/add period closed. I thanked her for her advice and told her I am extremely interested in the course topic, and I feel I can handle it, so I will stay. I left that day feeling frustrated that because of my young age I was being judged as not being capable. I decided not to let the situation get to me and give it my all. After about a month had passed since the professor pulled me aside and we had submitted our first writing assignment, again the professor asked me to stay after class. At the end of the class, she said that she had to apologize to me because she had judged my capabilities by my young age, but in fact, my assignment was one of the best. In that moment, I was so proud of myself for pushing through and not letting the thoughts of others bring me down.

When I first graduated from law school, I was ready to conquer the world. But I quickly found myself running into walls. I applied for several entry-level positions and kept falling short because I didn't have at least three years of experience. I thought to myself, how could a position be entry-level but require a minimum of three years of experience? How was I to gain the experience if no one would give me a chance? With every rejection, I began to doubt myself more and more. Had I made a mistake by going to law school? Was it all for nothing?

Then one day, my fiancé at the time asked me, "Why don't you open your own practice?" I thought to myself, Me? *Open my own practice?* I am not a business owner; my family is not full of business owners; can I even do this? I need to work for someone first, and then, years later, I can open a business. How can I do this straight out of the gate?

Why did I believe I had to work for someone first? Because that is what I was taught, that the only way to gain experience is by working for someone else first to show you the ropes. But is this the only way to do things? I learned all the tools and skills I need to practice law in law school. I gained experience by working in the law clinics in law school, so I do know what I am doing. There is no rule in the regulations of the law license that requires me to work for someone else before opening my own practice. So yes, I could do this. The only thing truly holding me back was my inner voice and self-doubt. I decided to quiet the negative noise from within and bet on myself. I told my fiancé, "Okay, yes, I am going to start my own business."

Throughout my career, I have felt like I was stuck in the muck, and I was simply waiting for the "right" time to act. Whether it was because I was waiting to start a family, or to be settled in my career, or even to find the right partner, the timing aspect played a critical part in determining when I would start living my dreams. However, I realized that timing should be used more as an element in making strategic business decisions, and it should not be used as a barrier to taking action. So, to tap into the universe's abundant resources, one must not only believe and manifest that there is abundance, but one must also create a system for obtaining one's goals and desires.

One of the systems that works well for me is simply to start—begin the task, the job, the call, the email, the conversation, take the steps into the unknown, and take actions towards whatever it is you are trying to achieve. I have been hesitant to take so many first steps that I quickly realized this was a bottleneck for achieving many things. For example, I used to think, "How would I, a first-generation, Black, Hispanic, female, who is chronically ill and grew up in an all-White town in central Massachusetts, have any chances of becoming a lawyer in America, let alone open my own law firm?" This privilege of practicing law is only reserved for 1% of Americans! The cards are clearly stacked against me. But rather than focusing on my perceived weaknesses, I focused on my capabilities and how I could use them to make this a reality.

The first step was to simply start. In law school, I tailored my curriculum to learn as much as I could about this country's laws and governing bodies and focused my extracurriculars on being more involved with my community and participating in the law clinics where, as students, we had the opportunity to take on legal cases. Then, after completing Law school, I still had to pass the licensing exam. I did not have money for the most expensive test prep courses or tutoring services, so I thought to myself, can I even do this? People who take the top course fail all the time. How am I going to pass? Well, I studied as I could. I tried following the steps that everyone around me was taking because I thought Oh, if everyone is taking these popular test prep courses, then it must be what I need to do as well. I went through the motions and took the exam and failed multiple times. After this, I thought to myself, well, do I give up, and all the money I spent on school and test prep would just be a waste? Or, do I block out all the noise and study for the exam my way and try something tailored more to my method of learning and doing things? I chose not to give up and to try things my way. I found a local small group with a one-on-one component study program and signed up. I thought this is my time, I took the exam again and this time I passed, I PASSED! I did it, I accomplished my dream of becoming a licensed attorney and the best part of it all was that I did it by trusting myself. When I stopped trying to do things how others said I should and I did things based on what works best for me, I succeeded.

Now, I have passed my exam, I am licensed, and I am ready to get to work, but I have no job. I applied to many different positions, went to several interviews, but was not getting hired. No one would give me a chance. Once again, I felt I was being judged without being known because of my age, and possibly lack of experience, although I had a lot of experience, just not more than 5 years of it, which was what most of the job openings were requiring, even though these were entry-level positions. So here I am facing another roadblock. Do I look for a job outside of the legal field and give up? That was not an option for me after all the struggles and hard work I refused to give up, so I decided to go at it alone and open my own practice.

THE IMPORTANCE OF CREATING NETWORKS

I have decided to open my own practice, but now what? I had no idea where to begin. What resources I had available to me, so I decided to start asking around. I joined a few bar associations and looked through their website for tools and resources. I talked with other solo practitioners and learned a little bit of what worked and didn't work for them. Then I took all these different pieces of information and began building my own systems and processes. I learned that even when you feel that you do not have the time, investing your time to connect with the community around you pays off in big dividends. They can help you connect with new opportunities, solve problems that you are having difficulty solving, and, most importantly, help you feel like you belong in this universe and that you are not alone.

DON'T GIVE UP

Something I always need to remind myself, especially when I am feeling defeated and doubting myself, is that the journey is not a straight line. There will be highs and lows and there may be some extremely bumpy seasons, but the only time you fail is when you give up. It is okay to make mistakes; that is how we learn. The important thing is not to let the mistake control your narrative.

I have made mistakes along the way in establishing and growing my legal practice. I started doubting my abilities, my capabilities, my knowledge. I started feeding into the negative and limiting thoughts assigned to me by others. I am too young to do this, Hispanics are not meant for this career, but then just as I find myself being consumed by these thoughts and gasping for air, I stand firm and say NO, this is not true, even the most experienced entrepreneurs make mistakes it is a part of life. Did I learn from the mistake? Yes, did I own the mistake and fix it? Yes... so no, it is not the end of the world, and I am not less than because I made a mistake, I am stronger because I learned from it and continued my journey, and so can you.

ADVICE THAT CHANGED MY LIFE

Don't read into situations, control the narrative, and interpret things from your point of view. It is important to stay true to yourself in the end and not let others' thoughts and beliefs determine who you are. You know who you are and the type of person you strive to be, and that is all that matters; we know best for ourselves. You will not be able to make everyone like you or your work, but that does not mean that you are bad at what you do and that you do not provide excellent service. Those people who do not like you have their own personal limitations and issues, and it is important not to take it personally and to make sure that they do not control the narrative of your story and journey you do. Lastly, don't be afraid of being "rubbed", that's how you become polished. People will always have an opinion and unsolicited advice. The important thing to do is take what works for us and learn from the positive thoughts and throw away the rest. We can only control how we choose to react to difficult situations, and with difficult people, we cannot control others. Therefore, it is important to remember to take a cooling-off period at times before responding to a negative statement or a difficult situation.

Biography

Karyn R. Sanchez, Esq., is a Tax and Immigration Attorney. She represents clients against the Internal Revenue Service, the Massachusetts Department of Revenue, United States Citizenship and Immigration Services (USCIS), the Department of Homeland Security (DHS), and the Executive Office of Immigration Review (EOIR).

As an attorney, Karyn also assists clients in business formation, tax preparation, partnership agreements, bylaws formation, business plan creation, financial analysis, and creating financial reports, to name a few. She is a member in good standing of the Massachusetts and New York Bars.

Karyn enjoys serving her fellow Latino community and the Worcester residents. She resides in Worcester and is invested in her work and her community.

Karyn is devoted to her family. She enjoys spending time with her husband and children, traveling together and soaking in the world and all it has to offer.

Karyn R. Sanchez
info@masstaxcorp.com

EMBRACING MY ENGLISH JOURNEY: TRANSFORMING CHALLENGES INTO OPPORTUNITIES

LEONELA GONZALEZ-FOGARTY

"Find your way, no matter what."

DEDICATION

I dedicate these words to all women professionals and entrepreneurs around the world—especially my fellow Latinas—who haven't found their voice in English yet. The time to overcome the fear of speaking is NOW. Transform every obstacle. Find your way no matter what.

I was born and raised in Venezuela and became an educator thanks to an amazing elementary school, Asociación para una Nueva Educación, where learning meant exploring, discovering, and expressing ideas. That foundation prepared me for my greatest challenge: Arriving in the U.S. with zero English and enrolling in a master's program in Education Computer and Technology at the University of Hartford. Even though I couldn't speak or understand English, I never doubted that I would make it.

I was teaching Education at the Universidad Metropolitana, one of the best universities in the country in Caracas, and saw a flyer in one of the bulletin boards offering a master's in educational computing and technology in Connecticut. I got very excited and felt a strong energy inside me that said, "This for you." It was the late '90s, right before the year 2000. Everyone in Venezuela was talking about Y2K and how "computers would explode." I didn't really understand it—computers were almost nonexistent in our schools. But one thought hit me: *A teacher who doesn't speak English or know computers will be disconnected from the world. That realization marked the beginning of my English journey.*

When I began my English journey at the age of 27 in 1997, I couldn't have imagined that I had fifty percent of what I needed to complete it. I went to study English at a language program offered by Colorado University in Denver. I knew I needed to immerse myself in the language to be able to speak the language. My godmother, a doctor from Venezuela, had also learned

English as an adult to complete her master program, so she told me that I needed to move away from Spanish at the beginning and immerse myself in English as much as I could. I followed her advice and went to Colorado to immerse myself in the language.

Once I arrived, I felt out of my comfort zone in many ways. I lived with a host family and didn't hangout with Spanish speakers to avoid speaking Spanish. The language program was traditional, heavily rooted in grammar and memorization practices. Since I have always been a good student, I did my best and got excellent grades. I did everything my English teachers told me to immerse myself in the language. I thought I could learn English quickly if I just studied hard enough, but I was wrong.

One afternoon, after completing four intense months of study, I decided to test my English. I went to McDonald's to order a combo and realized I couldn't communicate. The cashier asked me, "For here or to go?" and I couldn't understand. I froze trying to find the answer in my head and quickly replied to what I thought he was asking me. I said "No, I am from Venezuela." Thinking that he wanted to know where I was from, but it didn't make sense to me. I realized I was in trouble. I had only four more months to study to be ready to speak and express my ideas in my first master program and I still couldn't order a combo.

After my McDonald's experience, I had a heart-to-heart talk with myself and admitted that the traditional methods didn't work for me. I had a problem and needed to change the strategy. It wasn't easy. I realized that I was afraid to talk, especially with native speakers. My father always told me not to give up and try another way until I made it. I approached this language challenge the same way I approach triathlons, running marathons, and any other challenge in my personal/professional career. I changed the strategy and looked for help to solve it.

I asked the language program for new strategies. They suggested to pair-up and talk with native speakers who wanted to learn Spanish. That advice was a game changer. I found an American neighbor who became my first language partner and, later, my friend. We practiced talking every day on walks, during commutes, and over coffee. My fluency and confidence talking began to flow naturally. We practiced consistently for four months so when the time came to begin my master's program, I could finally communicate with professors and classmates, even though I was still nervous to talk. I could understand more and make myself understood.

Facing the fear of talking with native speakers was a hard reality because I kept thinking that if I learned the grammar and vocabulary perfectly I would be able to talk more. By talking to my friend about things I was interested in and things she was interested in, I no longer focused on saying things perfectly. I embraced this new process and went out of my way to talk to native speakers. It wasn't easy, but it worked.

No one had told me that my life experiences, my professional background, and my ability to face challenges were my valuable resources in learning a language. Years later, while studying for my second master's degree in applied linguistics at UMass Boston, my Harvard professor, the late Pepi Leitsina, said something that confirmed what I had already discovered: "Adult second language learners can learn to speak English faster than children—in just one year." Adults bring a full knowledge of the world, communicate effectively in their native language, and have the ability to set goals, create plans, and find strategies to reach them.

That experience taught me that immersion and real conversation, not grammar drills, build true fluency. While earning my first degree, I worked in the computer lab as a teacher assistant, so I had daily immersion and connection with Americans pushing me to communicate. Then, I moved to Boston, worked as a Spanish teacher in a two-way bilingual program in Framingham, Massachusetts, while studying my program in Applied Linguistics. I had the opportunity to enroll in a second master's program thanks to the town of Framingham that believes in high-quality education. This second master's opened a new world for me in my personal and professional career—the fascinating world of languages and culture.

By the time I was in Framingham, I had been exposed to and immersed in English for almost two and a half years with the language, but still needed practice. I could engage in conversations and express myself, but I was still translating in my head and working on my confidence. Since I was immersed in Spanish during the day teaching fourth graders, I asked my Venezuelan and Mexican roommates to speak with me in English to maintain my fluency. At first it felt strange to speak English with them, but I changed my mind set and imagined they were "gringos" (this term has a positive meaning between Latinos) to force me to talk. I knew my brain needed more. We were disciplined, encouraging, and created a safe space to practice, make mistakes, and grow. Their support was crucial to gaining confidence and mastering real-life English conversations.

Becoming a bilingual and multicultural teacher opened new opportunities. I returned to Venezuela in 2003 to teach in bilingual schools such as Colegio Guayamurí in Margarita Island and Escuela Campo Alegre in Caracas, an American international school. Working with local Venezuelan English teachers, American educators, and multicultural students expanded my teaching experience and perspective. The importance of connecting with students' personal and multicultural background stories and using the language in context for a specific purpose was key to guiding them to successfully communicate in another language. I realized that the confidence piece and daily exposure was key. Students needed to feel safe and comfortable in my classes and our school environments in order to speak English. These years in Venezuela strengthened my new career as a bilingual, multicultural, and language teacher.

While teaching at Escuela Campo Alegre, I noticed that many of the local Venezuelan staff couldn't communicate in English, even after years of working in an English-speaking environment. Most programs were either too expensive or ineffective. I started volunteering to teach English to security guards who wanted to talk to American teachers and parents. Their progress inspired me. I saw clearly that adults learn best when they connect their learning to who they already are—their strengths, experiences, and goals.

With these new experiences in mind about adult learning, I looked for a professional development course in Bangkok. In Venezuela we had many students from Asia, so I wanted to better understand their culture and countries where they were from. I began my TOEFL training, the American training to get the certification to teach English as a foreign language to adults. My interest in teaching adults started to develop even more.

We also had students from Europe, but the certificate for teaching adults in Europe, The CELTA, is a little different. So, I decided to go to Dublin to take another training in adult English as a second language to be better prepared to begin teaching adults, which was my new area of teaching interest.

These two training programs helped me to better understand the process of teaching English as a second language to adults. I taught teenagers in public schools in Bangkok and adult immigrants from all over the world in Dublin, each place adding new lessons about language, culture, and the power of language to connect with each other in a safe space. I noticed that both training sessions were still focused on grammar. I decided to teach differently, emphasizing conversation and personal connection based on who they already were and encouraging them to talk first about how their experiences in their home countries can help them in their new realities in new cities using the new language.

I can still remember a class I taught in Dublin when a talented artist and a business owner who couldn't talk in my class were finally able to connect. Even though the grammar wasn't perfect, they were able to communicate about what mattered to them. My adult students began to lose their fear of speaking as they shared stories about their lives and work. They realized, as I had years earlier, that English is not learned—it is *lived*.

In 2015, after more than twenty years of experience teaching and learning in the field of education, languages, and multiculturalism, I moved back to Boston with a new purpose: to create an English immersive conversation program for adult professionals, like me, who needed fluency to advance in their careers and lives. I knew traditional ESL methods weren't enough. I felt a call to do something different to solve the problem of teaching adult second language learners. Real immersion, conversation, and connection were key. Boston, the city that had once opened doors for me, became the birthplace of my new dream.

I began teaching Latino professionals using an immersive, conversation-based approach that focused on building confidence, self-awareness, and real-life communication in the Boston area. Students began speaking naturally and expressing who they truly were. Soon after, I joined Tufts University as an ESL instructor and volunteer coordinator for a preparatory program for international students in 2017. Their greatest struggle was fear—fear of speaking, fear of mistakes. I decided to design experiences that encouraged them to use English in real contexts. They volunteered in after-school programs, produced podcasts at a local radio station, and took cooking classes taught by Tufts' chefs. They practiced English while living it, and as they connected with others, their fluency blossomed.

In 2020 when the pandemic hit, I continued teaching online and realized how powerful virtual learning could be. Around that time, I joined an Instagram workshop with Venezuelan entrepreneur Verónica Ruiz del Viso, who inspired me to expand my teaching beyond the classroom in this new digital area. The digital world opened new doors, and my dream evolved into a life project and business: English for Life (E4L).

I started teaching my Venezuelan family and friends who were spread around the world and needed to speak English in their new cities and working environments. Then I began teaching entrepreneurs and professionals in the Massachusetts area. Without realizing it, I created a methodology with three key pillars—connect, immerse, transform—rooted in applied linguistics and two decades of experience teaching and learning across Venezuela, Thailand, Ireland, and the United States. English for Life empowered Hispanic and Latino professionals to overcome their fear of speaking English through immersive conversations professionally, culturally, and context-oriented programs. I have seen that no matter our age, our brain still follows the same natural stages of language acquisition—listening, understanding, speaking, fluency—but as adults, we have the advantage of knowledge, motivation, and purpose.

Learning English as an adult requires courage, consistency, and curiosity. Fluency is not a race, it is a relationship with the language. Real progress happens when we connect with our dreams, practice daily, and turn challenges into opportunities.

Now, in my mid-fifties, English has given me a second career, a business, and a renewed purpose. Through English for Life, my mission is to help to reduce the gap of Latino professionals and entrepreneurs across Massachusetts whose English is still a barrier to fully integrate in their new realities and culture. They need help to transform fear into confidence, silence into conversation, and dreams into action. Every day, I meet talented people who have the skills but hesitate to speak. I believe English for Life can play a key role in closing the ESL gap in our workforce and supporting economic growth across the state. As Founder and CEO of my own journey, I am committed to helping others embrace their English language journeys to transform their challenges into opportunities.

If you are a Latina professional, entrepreneur, or business owner still afraid to speak English, remember this: You already have half of what you need. The rest comes from embracing the challenge and creating an opportunity through practice, connection, and courage. The world of opportunities is limitless.

ADVICE THAT CHANGED MY LIFE

Since I was a child, my father always told me, "If you have a problem, fix it. If something doesn't go the way you want, find a way to make it right. Every problem has a solution—you just need to find your way, no matter what."

As a little girl, I remember feeling a bit frustrated by that advice. I was too young to understand its true meaning, yet somehow, I always tried my best to solve things on my own. As I grew older, his words became my mantra, especially when I decided to study abroad in the United States—the first in my family to do so. That goal brought challenges I could never have imagined, and my father's wisdom guided me throughout my personal and professional journey.

It may sound like a simple phrase, but it holds profound power. When you truly embrace it and apply it to any situation, you grow. You develop new abilities and strengths you never knew you had.

Learning English as an adult and completing my first master's degree transformed my life and continues to open doors I once thought impossible. My father's advice still lives within me, especially in moments of uncertainty or change.

I hope this same advice inspires you as it did me. Whatever problem or challenge you are facing, remember, find your way, no matter what.

Biography

Leonela Gonzalez-Fogarty is a Venezuelan American with a Bostonian heart. She is an educator, linguist, language consultant, immersive English coach, and founder of English for Life (E4L). With over 28 years of experience, she helps Hispanic/Latino professionals and entrepreneurs overcome the fear of speaking English through immersive programs, empowering them to be themselves, connect with American culture, and unlock their full potential.

A lifelong learner, passionate about teaching in multicultural environments, she continually innovates to help students reach their potential. Leonela believes English is more than a language—it's a path to limitless opportunities that develop our human potential. She proudly calls herself a **CHO**—a specialist in turning every **CH**allenge into an **O**pportunity.

In 1997, she moved to the U.S. to pursue a master's degree in educational computing and technology—arriving without speaking a word of English. Her personal transformation sparked her passion for language acquisition, especially in adult learners, leading her to work in Venezuela, Thailand, Ireland, and the U.S., including Tufts University.

In 2015, she returned to Boston to create an innovative method challenging myths about learning English as an adult. In 2020, she founded English for Life to help Latinas communicate confidently, expand their potential, and close the ESL gap in Massachusetts.

Leonela Gonzalez-Fogarty

leonela@english4lnetwork.com

https://connectenglishforlife.com/

www.instagram.com/english4lnetwork/

www.linkedin.com/in/leonela-gonzalez-fogarty-03493652/

OPENING DOORS, TURNING PAGES: MY
JOURNEY FROM ARECIBO TO AUTHORSHIP

MARGARITA L. PEREZ

"Believe in your voice and your story."

DEDICATION

I lovingly dedicate this story to my daughters, Leticia and Sofia, and my son, David. Your endless support and encouragement mean more to me than words can express. Every time I sit down to write, your faith in me gives me strength, and your kind words keep me going.

Thank you for always being there, for your patience, your love, and for helping me find just the right words when I get stuck. I couldn't do this without you.

Hola! My name is Margarita L. Perez, born on October 10, 1958, in the beautiful town of Arecibo, Puerto Rico. To family and friends, I'm Maggie. I am a daughter, sister, wife, grandmother, and aunt—but I am also an Erotic Romance author, a storyteller of love, passion, and imagination.

My love for stories began in high school, when my twin sister and I would wander the aisles of the Worcester Public Library. Those shelves held entire worlds of romance waiting to be discovered. Every Friday, we would check out as many books as we could carry, eager to lose ourselves in the lives of heroes and heroines who loved fiercely and fearlessly. I can still remember the thrill of opening a fresh book, the scent of the paper, and the sense of stepping into a new adventure. Those library visits became more than just entertainment—they were comfort, connection, and a way of adjusting to life in a new country after our move from Puerto Rico. Each story sparked curiosity, adventure, and a quiet dream that one day, I might create love stories of my own.

Many years later—now married, with three children, and working full-time—I began to feel a restless tug at my heart, a sense that there was something more I could do, something different and meaningful that I wanted for myself. Life was busy and full, with responsibilities at home, at work, and for my family, yet this feeling would not let me rest.

In 2008, for many consecutive days, a story lingered in my mind, persistent and vivid, refusing to fade no matter how busy my schedule or how tired I felt. I felt an almost urgent, unstoppable impulse to write it, to bring it into the world, but I was filled with doubt. I didn't know the first thing about writing a novel, and English was my second language. Yet, strangely, the story came to me fully formed in English, as if it had its own life, waiting for me to give it words. That tension between excitement and uncertainty made the story feel even more alive, and I knew I couldn't ignore it any longer.

I would later realize just how much that moment changed the course of my life—the day I casually mentioned to my coworkers during lunchtime that I had a story in my head that I wanted to write. I expected a polite nod or a smile, but instead, I was met with encouragement and excitement. They all immediately urged me to stop thinking about it and just start writing, insisting that I already had what it took to bring my story to life. Their words planted a seed of confidence in me, a spark that I would carry forward as I embarked on the uncertain, thrilling journey of becoming a writer. That simple lunchtime conversation, which might have seemed insignificant to anyone else, became a turning point in my life—the first real push that made me believe my dream of writing could actually become a reality.

I also realized that reading romance books had been my escape from some of the chaos at home. Working full-time with children and a house, I didn't have much time to read, but I still read a book once in a while. Reading sparked my imagination and helped me create love stories in my head.

By 2008, I was still thinking about that story but didn't know what to do with it. One day, in the cafeteria at work, I mentioned it again to my coworkers, and they encouraged me to just start writing. Their words gave me the confidence to try. It was the best and simplest advice I ever received. Still, I thought it was crazy of me to believe I could actually write a romance book—so I didn't do anything for a while.

Days later, I couldn't stop thinking about my story. I took their words to heart and decided to start writing. But there was an obstacle: I didn't know anything about writing a novel. I worked full-time, had a home, children, and a grumpy husband. My life was full as it was—but I was determined to learn how to write.

As English was my second language, I knew I faced a big challenge. I had never taken any creative writing classes in college, so I started researching online about how to write a novel. After many days of thinking about it at home and at work, I made the decision to start researching everything I could find about writing fiction.

Since my only free time was during lunch and breaks at work, I began Googling everything possible about writing— especially romance. I learned how to build a scene, describe settings, develop characters, and make them feel real. I printed everything I found and put it in a binder to study, highlighting sections and jotting notes in the margins. That binder became my personal textbook, my guide to a new world of possibilities. The excitement I felt was incredible, as if each page of research brought me one step closer to making my dream real.

After months of research, I finally pushed myself to start writing. It wasn't easy—I questioned everything I wrote and rewrote many scenes—but I loved it. Despite all the challenges at home and work, it took me two years to finish writing my first romance novel. It was one of my greatest struggles and one of the most rewarding accomplishments of my life.

In January 2010, my world shattered when I lost my five-month-old granddaughter, Adelina, Sudden Infant Death Syndrome (SIDS). The grief was unbearable, a heavy weight that seemed impossible to lift. Amid the sorrow of the funeral, a small flicker of hope appeared. I connected with one of my sisters-in-law's husbands, a man whose work involved editing articles for his company. When I spoke to him about my book, he offered to help edit it—a lifeline of support in the midst of my heartbreak. His guidance and encouragement transformed my fragile story into something polished and meaningful, giving me a reason to keep moving forward despite the pain.

Eager to share my story with the world, I dove into researching how to get my book published. I discovered that finding a literary agent was the golden key to reaching a traditional publisher. Each agent had their own unique submission requirements, and it took months of careful searching to find the right ones to contact. Balancing full-time work and family life, I began sending out my letters, one by one, with hope in my heart. After months of silence and rejections, a breakthrough finally came—a literary agent responded, expressing genuine interest in my book. I was over the moon! The excitement of knowing someone believed in my story fueled me with unstoppable energy and renewed determination.

Soon she asked me to send money for editing. Not knowing better, I sent it—only to later learn that you should never pay an agent upfront. A hard but valuable lesson learned.

While waiting for her reply, I made the decision not to pause my creative journey—I dove straight into writing my second book. Progress was slow at first, with moments of doubt and frustration, but this time I felt a growing sense of confidence in my abilities. I immersed myself in research, studying new techniques and exploring ways to deepen my characters and plots. Each day brought small breakthroughs, and I found myself not only improving my craft but also discovering new story ideas that fueled my imagination and excitement. The process became as much about learning and growing as it was about putting words on the page.

In July 2012, my world shifted when I was let go from my job. At first, it felt like a devastating blow, but thankfully, our finances were stable enough for me to embrace an unexpected opportunity: to stay home and write full-time. Fueled by determination, I poured my heart into my second book, completing it in 2014. Still waiting on the elusive literary agent, I made a bold decision—to take control of my dreams and self-publish through Amazon Kindle Direct Publishing (KDP). The process was slow, filled with challenges and moments of doubt, but step by step, I navigated it with persistence and the guidance of KDP support. Finally, on September 17, 2014, my first book was officially published. Holding it in my hands, seeing my words come to life for the world to read, was a moment of triumph—a pinnacle of pride and proof that my dream was real.

I continued writing and completed my third book a year later. Wanting a more guided process, I found a self-publishing company to help publish my next book in August 2015. I eventually self-published a total of eight erotic romance novels, including the one that had originally been with the literary agent. My last book was published in September 2020.

Self-publishing was both exciting and heartbreaking. I was proud of my work but disappointed that my books didn't generate income. That caused many arguments with my husband, especially as I used some of my 401(k) and pension funds to pay for publishing. In 2022, I decided to take a break from self-publishing—but not from writing.

In 2023, I connected with AMR Anthologies through Facebook and met Andrea, whose encouragement was incredible. She introduced me to the world of anthologies, and I participated in six. Two of them became Best-Selling and International Best-Selling anthologies.

My life as an author has been challenging and difficult, but also the happiest time of my life. I never gave up on my dream. I never imagined myself as an author—especially a Latina woman writing in English—but I am. I have published nine books and six anthologies, and I am very proud of my accomplishments. I wouldn't change anything, not even the financial struggles. Writing has made my life better.

I've spoken with many young adults who ask me about my books and how to start writing. I always tell them: just start writing. Don't let anyone discourage you. If I—a 15-year-old Puerto Rican girl who moved to the U.S. in 1973 without knowing any English—could learn to write books in English, then anyone can.

These past two years have been a learning experience as a Latina writer. I've met so many wonderful Latina authors through Empowering Latina Leaders Affirmation (known as ELLA). The encouragement I've received has been amazing, and I feel so welcomed. I hope I can also encourage and support others in return.

ADVICE THAT CHANGED MY LIFE

When I first became interested in writing, I had no mentors to guide me, nor did I personally know any romance authors. My coworkers, however, knew I loved reading romance novels because I often shared my thoughts about the books I read. Eventually, I began hinting about my desire to write my own stories.

One day during lunch, after I once again expressed my interest, my coworkers gave me the simplest yet most powerful advice: *"Just start writing your story."* That encouragement was all I needed to begin my journey as a writer.

The advice I now share with aspiring writers is this: **start writing.** Surround yourself with positive people who support your goals. Seek out writing groups where you can share your passion, meet other writers, and gain encouragement. Writing takes time, patience, and effort, but the joy of creating your own story is incredibly fulfilling.

Never let negativity stop you. Don't worry about what others may say, and don't allow anyone to discourage you from writing. Believe in your voice and your story, and keep going—because the world needs it.

Biography

Margarita L. Perez was born in Arecibo, Puerto Rico, in 1958. She has a twin sister, Lourdes, along with siblings Hector, Manuel, Jose, Nexsa, and Rosa.

In 1973, her family moved to Worcester, Massachusetts. Margarita has been married to her husband, David, for 45 years, and together they have three children—Leticia, Sofia, and David. She is also a proud grandmother to eight grandchildren: Ricardo, Evan, Adelina, Alejandro, Fernando, Emmit, Luciano, and Gabrielle.

Margarita earned her Associate Degree in Business Management from Quinsigamond Community College. In 1981, she began her professional career at Paul Revere Companies as a Premium Collection Specialist. Over the span of more than 30 years, she held several positions within the company, concluding her career there as an Underwriting Specialist in IDI Business Operations before retiring in July 2012.

Her passion for writing began in 2008 on a part-time basis, and by 2012 she embraced it full-time. Writing is her true calling, though she also enjoys Latin music, dancing, reading, and sports. A devoted fan of the Boston Red Sox, she brings the same energy and passion to her personal interests as she does to her craft.

Under the pen name **Margy Millet,** she writes contemporary, paranormal, vampire, fae, and sci-fi erotica romance. She has published nine standalone books and contributed six short stories to six different anthologies.

Margarita L. Perez

margymillet@gmail.com

www.margymillet.com

Instagram: @lourdesm1958

Facebook: Margy Millet

SPEAKING FROM THE HEART: HOW MY BILINGUAL VOICE BECAME MY SUPERPOWER

MARÍA GONZÁLEZ

"Haz bien y no mires a quien."

DEDICATION

To Aliyah, and every young Latina reading this, You come from strong, brilliant, bilingual women who lead with courage. Your voice is powerful, never doubt it. Speak with purpose, be curious, ask bold questions, and tell your story even when it trembles. Lead with love. You never need to shrink to belong; you belong because you're you. If a room can't hold your brilliance, speak so passionately they redesign it. You are my legacy and our limitless future.

"You smell like a candle," George, my significant other for 11 years.said to me one evening with the sweetest of smiles.

I spun around with squinted eyes. "Like a burnt candle?"

"No! No," he quickly added, laughing. "Like one of those beautiful candles you light around the house. You smell amazing."

"Well," I replied, half-joking and fully serious, "maybe next time lead with the compliment."

And just like that, a perfect lesson on communication unfolded in our living room. Communication isn't just about words. It's about clarity, timing, tone, and, most importantly, intention. As a bilingual Latina who has walked through both boardrooms and barrios, I've learned to turn the art of communication into my superpower.

THE VOICE THAT CARRIES ME

I was born in vibrant Ponce, Puerto Rico, where voices echo through alleyways like music, where everyone talks over one another, lovingly, passionately, always loudly. That's where I learned to speak my first language, Spanish.

When we moved to the mainland U.S.A., I had to learn English quickly. English wasn't just another language; it was the key to survival in school and social circles. But it didn't replace Spanish; it nestled right next to it. I grew up code-switching without even realizing it, flipping effortlessly between "*¿Qué pasó?*" and "What's going on?"

Some people think accents are barriers. I believe accents are bridges proof that we have crossed oceans and cultures and still carried our voices with us. My accent tells a story long before I open my mouth to explain who I am. It announces: "I am both." I am from here, and I am from there. I am English and Español. I am powerfully, and beautifully bilingual.

PROFESSIONAL WITH A PURPOSE

When I reflect on how communication has shaped my path, I think about the journey that brought me from government halls in Massachusetts to founding my consultancy, M&A Supplier Diversity Consultants. In my two decades of public service, particularly at the Massachusetts State House, in the Office of Access & Opportunity, the Operational Services Division, and the Supplier Diversity Office, I have learned that the most significant policy changes occur when people feel heard. True inclusion doesn't start with data or PowerPoint slides. It begins with real conversations.

When I launched my business, **M&A Supplier Diversity Consultants,** right after retirement in 2019, it wasn't just about offering a service; it was about **elevating voices.** Supplier diversity is more than a procurement initiative, it's a commitment to equity in the marketplace. It means **creating intentional opportunities for businesses owned by minorities, women, veterans, LGBTQ+ entrepreneurs, and people with disabilities** to compete fairly for corporate and government contracts.

Supplier diversity helps level the playing field for small

businesses that have historically been excluded from major supply chains. For the **business community of color,** it can be transformative, opening doors to contracts, mentorship, and resources that fuel growth and generational wealth. It's not charity; it's smart economics. Diverse suppliers bring innovation, agility, and deep community insight to the table, enriching the businesses that partner with them.

Supplier diversity is about opportunities, yes, but it's also about **listening,** listening to the business owner who has been told "no" a thousand times, and listening to companies that want to do better but don't know where to start. My job is to bridge those voices, to translate intention into action, and I do it fluently in English, in Spanish, and in the universal language of **equity.**

Communication is why I've helped more than 1,500 businesses access the supplier certification process and take advantage of procurement opportunities. I often speak the language of strategy, compliance, and community simultaneously.

PODCAST, PUBLIC SPEAKING, AND THE POWER OF PLAIN TALK

People are often surprised when they hear me speak on panels or listen to my podcast, *The Diversity Duo.* Maybe it's the accent, or maybe it's the passion, but I always speak plainly. I've learned that clarity is a form of kindness. Whether I'm mentoring a young entrepreneur through SCORE or discussing inclusive procurement with a corporate executive, I never dilute who I am to make someone else more comfortable.

You see, too many Latinas are told to "soften" their voices to speak less, to smile more, to blend in. I say: Speak up. Speak boldly. Speak bilingually, if that comes naturally to you. And please, never apologize for your accent. That's your grandmother's voice, your hometown, your story. That's your *power*.

Being Latina is not just an ethnicity; it's a rhythm. It's body language, facial expressions, storytelling around the dinner table, and that famous eyebrow raise from your Tía that says everything without saying a word.

Communication is culture, is how we connect, how we lead, how we love. I bring all of that into my business. When I mentor others, especially young Latinas, I encourage them to lean into their cultural communication styles. Don't try to strip your voice down to something sterile. Your authenticity will always outperform perfection.

This is why I love salsa dancing, gardening, and long walks, because communication isn't always verbal. It's in movement, in presence, in action. It's how you show up. And I show up fully. As a woman. As a Latina. As a bilingual leader who has never lost touch with the little girl from Ponce.

GEORGE AND THE CANDLE

Let me return to George and the candle for a moment, because it was more than just a funny moment; it was a revelation. When he said, "You smell like a candle," and I flinched, it reminded me that communication is a delicate matter. It's wrapped in memory, in bias, in how we've been spoken to before. He meant it kindly, but I needed to hear it clearly. And isn't that the truth for so many of us? We hear things through filters. We respond through past hurts or cultural lenses.

That's why I told him: "Next time, lead with the compliment." Because in life and business, the opening line matters. People remember how you made them feel first. Then they listen to the words.

George and I still laugh about it. But now, every time I light a candle, I think about how something so simple taught me another layer of what it means to communicate with love.

BILINGUALISM AS A SUPERPOWER

When people ask me what it's like to live in two languages, I tell them it's like being a superhero with dual vision. I see things others don't. I connect dots across cultures. I empathize more quickly, negotiate more effectively, and adapt more easily.

Throughout my career, this has enabled me to serve both clients and the community with nuance. I can sit in a high-level meeting one day, then coach a first-generation business owner the next.

Language isn't a barrier, it's a bridge. And when that bridge is built on respect, authenticity, and good communication, it can carry the weight of real change.

FINAL WORD

I never imagined that the voice I once felt insecure about the accent that made me repeat myself in meetings, the moments I hesitated to switch between English and Spanish, the loudness that some called "too much" would one day become the same voice that empowers others, signs contracts, mentors leaders, and speaks on stages. For a long time, I tried to soften it, to fit into rooms that weren't built with my cadence in mind. But in finding my confidence, I learned that what I once saw as flaws were actually my power.

Communication is not just how I navigate the world; it's how I shape it. Every word, every story, every "r" rolled or syllable spoken in Spanglish carries the history of who I am, and who I represent.

So yes, I smell like a candle. A bright, powerful, unmistakable flame that continues to light the way, not just for me, but for all the women who come after me.

And that, *mi querida lectora,* is the power of our voice.

ADVICE THAT CHANGED MY LIFE

"Never depend on another for your survival." That advice came from my mother, Adelina, and it became my compass. It taught me to develop my own financial independence, emotional resilience, and intellectual strength. It reminded me that support is a blessing, but self-sufficiency is power. I've carried those words

through every challenge, from navigating government systems to launching my own business. That advice didn't just shape my mindset; it shaped my mission.

The one advice I would share with you, the reader, is that clarity is a form of kindness, both to others and to yourself. Whether in business or personal relationships, speaking your truth with purpose and compassion opens doors, diffuses confusion, and builds lasting connections. Don't water yourself down to fit in. Be bold in your words, own your story, and trust that authenticity is the most magnetic force you have.

Biography

María González is the Founder and Principal of M&A Supplier Diversity Consultants, a Massachusetts-based firm committed to advancing equity through inclusive procurement strategies. A native of Ponce, Puerto Rico, Maria brings over two decades of experience in public service, including key roles in the Massachusetts State House, the Operational Services Division, and the Office of Access and Opportunity.

Since launching her consultancy in 2019, she has helped over 1,000 small and diverse businesses navigate certification processes and access procurement opportunities. Maria is a recognized expert in supplier diversity and regularly shares her insights as a keynote speaker, panelist, and co-host of *The Diversity Duo* podcast.

Appointed by Governor Maura Healey to the Supplier Diversity Office Advisory Board and the Board of Trustees at Bristol Community College, Maria also serves as Vice Chair of the Taunton Area Chamber of Commerce and as a Certified SCORE Business Mentor.

Beyond business, María is a passionate gardener, salsa dancer, dog mom, and proud vegetarian in a meat-loving family. Her life's work is centered around creating systemic change and opening doors for others.

María González

info@supplierdiversityconsultants.com

www.linkedin.com/in/masdc2019

MY PROFESSIONAL JOURNEY: DESTINY IS A
HARD THING TO RUN FROM

MONSERRATE RODRÍGUEZ COLÓN

—————

*"Truly successful decision-making relies on a balance
between deliberate and instinctive thinking."*
- Malcolm Gladwell

DEDICATION

My chapter is dedicated to my two sons, Hector Jr. and
Mason Quiñones, who witnessed their mother as I overcame

adversity, struggled maintaining a home and career, while finishing her degrees and certifications without a village for support. Their unconditional love sustained me through it all. I did it for you boys!

My professional journey has been a tapestry woven with ambition, uncertainty, resilience, and a persistent desire to help others find their own paths. In retrospect, I see how my parents' own story of survival in extremely difficult economic and social times immigrating to the mainland from Puerto Rico in the late sixties built in me the ambition to make the most of the opportunities this country had to offer. Their living example—raising a large family with only a third-grade education and limited English—showed me that faith, hard work, and hope lead to success. This roadmap of love for family, dedication to education, and willingness to do hard things with excellence propelled my career and caused me to receive much recognition.

Over the course of decades in public service, I've had the privilege of serving across sectors in Massachusetts that span education, the judiciary, and the executive branch. From my early days as a public-school teacher to senior leadership positions—including Commissioner of the Massachusetts Commission Against Discrimination—I've worked to advance equity and inclusion at every level. My path led me to deepen my commitment to community impact. Along the way, I was honored to receive appointments from six different governors, a testament to the trust placed in my leadership and vision. I am grateful for all these opportunities, especially coming from such humble beginnings. I owe all my success to the family that nurtured me and community of the south side of Framingham that raised me and the mentors who believed in me. My story is not only a timeline of roles and titles, but a collection of lessons earned through both adversity and achievement.

BEGINNINGS AND EARLY CHALLENGES

From the start my resources were few and role models in my own community nonexistent. There were few mentors in the public school system starting in the late sixties and seventies that could inspire and assist in seeking a college education. Learning English as a second language, like many immigrants, was not easy but I was able to advance through summer classes and graduated as a junior from high school. Thankfully, Mrs. Aaronson, an English as a second language teacher, was instrumental in helping many immigrant students who dreamed of higher education.

In those days a high school diploma and going to work in the many factories around town like our parents was good enough. Through Mrs. Aaronson's guidance I was able to submit college applications. I chose to attend the University of Massachusetts Amherst, mostly because it took me away from my sheltered family life and offered me a great financial aid package.

At a young age I desired to be exposed to a bigger world

view. I dreamt of being a revolutionary like Pedro Albizu Campos. I wanted to change the world and improve the lives of people in my community. Unfortunately, my mother, Eugenia Santos Rodríguez, never lived to see my success. She passed away when I was a sophomore in college. Shortly after, my father moved to Puerto Rico, and I did not see him for the next ten years. I was completely on my own and solely responsible for all my decisions. I had to rely on the breadcrumbs they left and the lessons they instilled in me to survive. At this point it was important for me to surround myself with people who would be a positive influence in my life.

FROM UNCERTAINTY TO EMPOWERMENT

Like many, my career began with more questions than answers. I stepped into the professional world with a bachelor's degree in education with a concentration in human services, which at the time was a new field of study. I had a lot of enthusiasm tempered by self-doubt, keenly aware of how much I needed to learn. I returned to Framingham and connected with some of my teachers who offered me the opportunity to work as a public-school teacher with English language learners and the special education department. It required adaptability, and I often found myself facing steep learning curves.

I went on to get certified as a social worker and worked several years as a social worker, both in the Department of Transitional Assistance as an Employment and Training Social

Worker, as well as a Family Advocate for the South Middlesex Opportunity Council supporting homeless families. Some of the first lessons I learned were to find opportunities to be creative, to discover my strengths, and to find ways to develop special projects. As a social worker I developed a partnership with the agency offering mental health services and began co-leading support groups for families living in the shelter program. Through these experiences I was led to apply for probation service which was a huge steppingstone in my career. There were moments when challenges seemed insurmountable, both in my professional and personal life, and I had to dig deep to find self-motivation and understanding of the system regardless of whether rejection or failure would follow. By this time, I had two young children and started a master's program. However, I never questioned my own capabilities or the fact that I could achieve better opportunities. It was important for me to be an example my kids could model after.

There were moments when the weight of professional and personal challenges demanded more than just endurance—they required a deep well of self-motivation, faith in God and a clear grasp of the systems I was navigating, even when rejection or failure stood as a constant threat. I knew I couldn't afford to falter; too many people were relying on me. But it was precisely within these defining struggles that I discovered the true meaning of perseverance. Every setback became a teacher, offering lessons in humility, growth, and the reality that progress is rarely a straight path. Through adversity, I cultivated resilience—not as a trait I was born with, but as a skill forged in the fire of experience.

LEARNING THROUGH EXPERIENCE

As I advanced, I leaned into taking on added responsibilities and filled the gap of services needed in the community. When I served as a probation officer, I became very involved with community partners and led round table discussions with local law enforcement officials, public school administrators, social service providers, and other public entities to bring a comprehensive approach to law enforcement and address recidivism. I was approved to lead, what was considered at the time, an innovative substance abuse support group for probationers in my courthouse. In addition, I volunteered to serve as community leader in an initiative started by Antonia Jimenez, who at the time was Special Assistant to Governor Paul Cellucci titled the Massachusetts Education Initiative for Latino Students (MEILS). I was recommended to this role by my administrative judge, the Honorable Luis Perez, who continues to be a great mentor and friend. I attribute this opportunity due to the work I was leading outside of the role of probation officer.

I was so successful in my community organizing efforts for the MEILS initiative in the town of Milford, Massachusetts, that I was a featured speaker at the MEILS summit where all the community organizers met and presented our outcomes to Governor Cellucci and Lieutenant Governor Jane Swift. My efforts led me to getting promoted to the next Special Assistant to Governor Cellucci when Ms. Jimenez advanced to another position.

I chose uncertainty rather than shying away from it. I was leaving a permanent position in probation to an appointed role in the governor's office. I sought out mentors, chipped away at courses to complete my master's degree, and embraced opportunities to lead even when I felt unprepared. Through trial and error, I developed a toolkit of skills and, more importantly, an openness to continual learning.

Promotion brought challenges I wasn't ready for, but my confidence from past successes made me believe that hard work would lead to success. Knowing that my mentors put trust in me gave me a boost to trust the process.

Working at the Executive Branch in the Governor's office I went from a paper driven system to computerized coordination for everything work related, which was a huge learning curve for me. Then, I learned the biggest lessons about who I wanted to become and how influential in public policy I wanted to be. I took the opportunity to expand the visibility and importance of state's Affirmative Market Program (AMP) and imprinted the mission to expand opportunities for women, minority-owned, and small businesses contracting with the state procurement system. Through my leadership many initiatives were developed that still are in practice, including requirement for ancillary use of certified companies and subcontracting requirements of large companies endeavoring to do business in the state.

Through my advocacy the Supplier Diversity Office was founded. I received national recognition for creating the Business-to-Business Mentoring Program, which also established opportunities for other state supplier diversity offices to mentor less developed state agencies. Massachusetts mentored the state of Missouri. My passion for mentoring was fueled by these initiatives.

At this stage and after nine years as Executive Director for the AMP, I wanted to increase my knowledge of diversity and inclusion in human capital. I successfully sought appointment to become the first Director of DEI at the Department of Correction and founded the Office of Diversity and Equal Opportunity, where I led the design and implementation of the department's first Diversity, Equity, and Inclusion model. For example, I created a succession planning program, staff cross-training opportunities, was awarded the first mediation grant given to a state agency from the Federal Mediation Conciliation Service offering 30 employees across the system to become certified mediators and a dedicated staff in my office to offer mediation services, drafted department policies to address anti-discrimination concerns, developed a comprehensive recruitment and retention agenda which increased representation for women and other unrepresentative groups in the workforce. This was one of the most rewarding and difficult roles of my career. I have always sought to leave an organization in a better state than when I started. Many initiatives that were created through my leadership are still in place, including mentoring programs for staff, the Commissioner's Diversity Advisory Committee, and the department's first internship program. One of my mentees, Janice Perez, is the current director of this office, which makes me very proud. I received national and state recognition for the many initiatives developed in my tenure from the American Correctional Association.

As a result of these innovative initiatives supported by DOC staff, managers, and senior leaders who trusted the process milestones and performance measures were achieved. After these successes, I was recommended as Commissioner for the Massachusetts Commission Against Discrimination (MCAD) where I continued my anti-discrimination work. This was another opportunity to leave a legacy and a path for others to follow and perhaps the next generation of leaders to see themselves represented and encouraged to take the road less traveled.

As Commissioner for MCAD I enforced federal and state anti-discrimination laws in employment, housing, credit, lending, education, and public accommodation. My jurisdiction included western, central, and southeast parts of the state. The trust bestowed upon me was an honor and privilege, which hopefully continues to provide pathways for inspiration.

I retired in June 2025 after nearly a decade as a commissioner, which I consider my capstone position. Six governors appointed me to state senior positions in their administrations, marking my developed skills, adaptation to changing environments, and reputation for strong people-driven leadership, resulting in effective policy development, compliance of mandates and laws, and creative solutions to public issues.

HELPING OTHERS AND FINDING PURPOSE

Some of my most rewarding moments still come from mentoring and supporting others, particularly women working in male-dominated work environments, such as public safety. I have had the privilege of guiding new team members as they navigated the uncertainties I once faced being the only female or Latina in the room. By sharing my own stories of doubt, perseverance, and triumph, I helped normalize the challenges inherent to professional growth and encouraged others to approach obstacles as opportunities.

Witnessing their successes—however small—reinforced the value of vulnerability and the power of collective learning. In helping others, I found deeper meaning in my work and a renewed sense of purpose. John C. Maxwell says, "You never really know something until you teach it to someone else."

Each achievement noted in this chapter is a testament to my persistence and the determination to embrace both failure and opportunity and to take risks in my career path. More importantly, each opportunity has been a chance to pay it forward, to support those who are just beginning their own journeys or who find themselves momentarily lost. Throughout my career, I have developed internship and mentoring programs for small, minority and women-owned business, employees, high school, and college students. I am a current member and co-chair of the University of Massachusetts Women into Leadership Program (UWil). In this capacity, working with young women who are making major decisions about their academic future where they might best fit in public policy and public careers that will lead them to be change makers has been one of the best experiences in my life. Having come from an economically disadvantaged family and community and now being able to guide the next generation of leaders is the ultimate full circle moment for me.

LOOKING AHEAD

I continue to share my experiences openly, believing that my story has the power to inspire, inform, and unite. The road has not always been easy, but I am grateful for every challenge, every doubt, every "no," every triumph—each has shaped the professional I am today and strengthened my resolve to help others grow alongside me. I continue to mentor and advise colleagues, former staff, mentees, and friends. My philosophy is that if my cup is full, I cannot receive new blessings. So, I must pour myself into others' dreams, future, and career success to grow as a leader but, most importantly, to give back to others, which is the best investment and legacy any human can leave behind.

Today I look forward to the new challenge of self-employment and having my own business. It's my turn to be an entrepreneur to continue serving using all the wisdom, knowledge, and experience from decades of leadership practice.

ADVICE THAT CHANGED MY LIFE

Leadership is not a title—it's a commitment to growth of self and others, to having integrity and impact. Over the years, I've learned that change begins with the individual. If you want to see transformation, you must first embody it. Leadership also requires boundaries; you cannot be both a leader and a friend. Clarity of role allows you to model the behavior you expect from others and to inspire through example.

The path is rarely linear. Sometimes, the best decision for the organization may not serve the individual, and circumstances will inevitably shape your course. Be nimble. Trust your instincts, especially when logic and intuition collide—but don't rush decisions that require reflection. Know your worth and the value you bring. Avoid making choices rooted in fear; instead, ground your decisions in data and purpose.

Leadership is collaborative. Share your vision boldly and bring others along to inspire meaningful change. Engage beyond your organization—be a bridge builder, a connector, and a learner. Seek guidance when needed; you don't have to carry every answer alone. Growth demands humility. Recognize areas for improvement and invest in your development through education and training.

Above all, remember, you are your greatest asset. Prioritize self-care and protect your work-life balance. When the moment calls for it, step beyond your formal role to fill gaps, gain insight, and grow. And never negotiate your future from a place of anxiety—lead with confidence, clarity, and conviction.

Biography

Monserrate "Monsi" Rodríguez Colón earned her bachelor of science in education with a concentration in human services from the University of Massachusetts Amherst and a master of science in public administration from Worcester State University. She is a licensed social worker, certified mediator, HRCI-licensed Human Resources professional, certified MCAD trainer and an alumna of the Harvard Kennedy School's Executive Education program in public leadership and diversity.

As a trailblazer, Monsi has spent most of her decades long career in executive senior leadership roles in state government influencing public policy in social justice and public safety. She is a former advisory board member for Worcester State University's Criminal Justice Department and currently serves as co-chair of the University of Massachusetts Amherst's Women into Leadership (UWiL) program, mentoring the next generation of women changemakers.

Monsi's outstanding achievements have earned multiple prestigious awards, including recognition from the National Institute of Corrections for leading the country's most transformative DEI correctional program where she helped create a roadmap for employer-based support for correctional officers. She also received national recognition during her tenure as the Commonwealth of Massachusetts Executive Director of the Affirmative Market Program (now Supplier Diversity Office) for designing one of the most innovative procurement systems in the country. She was a 2024 ALX 100 honoree and named the 2024 University of Massachusetts Alumni Randolph W. "Bill" Bromery Legacy in Civil Rights Awardee.

Monsi is the CEO of MRC Business and Consulting Services, LLC.

Monserrate Rodríguez Colón

mrcbusinessconsulting@gmail.com

www.linkedin.com/in/monserrate-rodriguez-colon

FROM BORINQUEN TO BOSS LADY

NIVIA J. PINA-MEDINA

"People will forget what you said, people will forget what you did, but people will never forget how you made them feel." -Maya Angelou

DEDICATION

To my parents, who gave me roots; to my husband, who gives me strength; and to my children, who give me wings.

I was raised in Puerto Rico by two artists who couldn't have been more different. My mother was strict, quiet, and always a bit mysterious—like she was holding back a novel's worth of stories behind her sewing machine. My father? The total opposite. He was warm, affectionate, endlessly helpful, and one of the most creative people I've ever known. He could fix anything with his hands and imagine everything with his heart. One could fix a zipper in under three minutes flat, and the other could rebuild an engine while helping me build a volcano for a science project—calm as ever, covered in grease, and loving every minute of it. I guess you could say I was destined to be both practical and creative—whether I liked it or not.

My mother was a master seamstress and weaver; her discipline was legendary in our home. She didn't need to raise her voice—one look was enough to bring me and my brother into line. But she had magic in her hands. She created beauty stitch by stitch, even when life didn't give her perfect fabric to work with. She had a very harsh childhood and only reached 8th grade because she had to work to help her sister finish school. But that woman understood the value of education more than anyone I've ever met. You could see the pain in her eyes for not being able to finish, even though she never said much about it. Her silence carried wisdom—and heartbreak.

My father, on the other hand, was more of an artist in spirit—someone who could create anything from scratch, whether it was fixing an engine or building something entirely new. He had a gift for problem-solving and making things work, often in the most creative ways. Despite their different personalities, my parents truly complemented each other. Where she brought structure and discipline, he brought warmth and imagination. Together, they formed a perfect balance of heart and hands.

Their artistry didn't come with applause or gallery shows. It came with sacrifice. They gave up comforts so my brother and I could live a childhood free from scarcity. I'll never forget how they stretched their time, money, and energy to make sure we participated in everything—from school plays to Girl Scouts, which played a big role in shaping who I am. Through it all, they passed down not just their skills, but their resilience, their integrity, and their love for Puerto Rico.

From early on, community service wasn't something we did—it was simply part of who we were. My parents didn't have much, but they always found a way to give—whether it was my mom sewing a neighbor's dress for free, or my dad fixing someone's broken machine just because it was the right thing to do. And it wasn't just them. I grew up surrounded by people who looked out for one another, who shared what they had, who showed up with food, tools, or laughter when someone was in need. There was a strong sense of *comunidad*—of shared responsibility and pride—that shaped how I saw the world. That foundation became the lens through which I would later lead, teach, serve, and build. I didn't just grow up in a household of artists—I grew up in a village of givers.

Growing up, I dreamed of becoming an architect. I would sketch houses with grand staircases and hidden courtyards, imagining a world I could help build. I was endlessly curious—science books, art classes, and puzzle games were my jam. But architecture meant leaving the island, and my mother's answer to that was a firm, loving "No." She wasn't about to let her daughter go off to study in another country, not under her roof—and, truthfully, we didn't have the means to send me. That reality didn't crush my dream; instead, it gave me the courage to explore different ways to make it possible. I started looking for scholarships, financial aid, and any opportunity that could one day fund my studies abroad.

So instead, I found ways to build differently. I became a chemist and then a special education teacher. I discovered that education is its own kind of architecture. You lay a foundation, nurture growth, and help shape futures.

I came to Boston to pursue graduate studies at Brandeis, full of hope and a suitcase packed with dreams—and sweaters. Finally able to leave! I still remember my first winter vividly: I stepped outside bundled in layers, but the cold sliced through me like a blade. The snow was unfamiliar, the silence unsettling, and the rhythm of life felt harsh. I had left behind a warm, loud, and familiar island where everyone greeted each other with a smile. Suddenly, I was in a fast-paced city where people rarely made eye contact, let alone conversation.

But more than the weather, it was the subtle and not-so-subtle reminders that I didn't belong that shook me. I encountered racism for the first time—dismissive comments, assumptions about my intelligence, my accent, or even my right to be in certain spaces. It was humbling and infuriating. I went from being articulate and confident to second-guessing every word I spoke.

Still, I didn't let it defeat me. I took it one day at a time, asking questions when I didn't know something, laughing at myself when I made mistakes, and building community wherever I could. Over time, I learned to navigate the trains, the culture, the expectations—and the biases. Slowly, Boston began to feel like home, not because it changed, but because I grew stronger. My Puerto Rican roots gave me the courage to grow new ones, and that made all the difference.

Amid all these changes, becoming a mother gave my journey new meaning. My children became my motor—everything I do is for them. I want my daughter to grow up knowing she can be strong, opinionated, and ambitious. I want her to see her voice as a tool, not a threat. And for my son to know that gentleness and strength can coexist. Motherhood didn't just push me to do more—it transformed the way I led in every aspect of my life.

I also poured my creativity into event planning, crafts, and eventually the restaurant businesses I run today with my husband, Héctor, who has been my partner not just in love but in purpose. Together, we've built more than just places to eat—we've created cultural spaces that celebrate identity, family, and resilience.

When we design a new restaurant, I get my chance to finally be the architect—picking colors, laying out the flow, creating environments that invite community.

As a restaurateur, I've had the privilege of hearing the stories of countless people from all walks of life. Coming from Puerto Rico—a beautiful island that is culturally rich but relatively homogeneous in terms of immigration—I was deeply moved by the lived experiences of those who left everything behind to start over in a new country. Their courage, their losses, their triumphs—those stories didn't just inspire me; they changed me. They've shaped how I lead, how I raise my children, and how I show up in the world. Today, I don't just serve food—I hold space for humanity, one story at a time.

I remember one afternoon after an event we hosted at the restaurant—a woman approached me with tears in her eyes. She told me that seeing a Latina business owner thriving in our city made her believe that she, too, could chase a dream she'd kept buried for years. I can still recall the way she held my hands as she spoke, her eyes shimmering with emotion. That moment stayed with me. It wasn't about the event, the food, or even the recognition—it was about the quiet ripple effect of simply showing up. That was when I realized I was poderosa. Not because I held a title or had all the answers, but because my presence helped someone else see what was possible. Power doesn't always roar. Sometimes it whispers through resilience, values, and the courage to keep going. If my journey can open even one door, then I'll wear the word poderosa with pride.

There was a time when clarity hit me hard—when my father suffered a fall at work and lost his job. Suddenly, our financial stability was shaken. We had to adjust, and I even had to change schools. But what didn't change was their effort to keep me in Girl Scouts, where I felt grounded, supported, and seen. That moment taught me about adaptation and strength through uncertainty.

When setbacks come—and they do often—I stay grounded in the present. I don't obsess over the long road. I keep doing what needs to be done today, even if that means pushing a goal back a little further. Progress isn't linear. It's made of little wins stacked with grit.

Change doesn't scare me anymore. I've learned to be flexible, to pivot, and to trust that even the detours serve a purpose. Complaining wastes energy. Moving forward conserves it.

When it comes to decision-making, I don't rush. I check in with myself—if something feels out of sync, I step back and listen. Intuition isn't loud, it's quiet. It speaks in gut feelings and emotional pulls. I've learned to trust that. I make decisions based on alignment, not impulse.

I try to balance power with grace by staying humble. I don't need to be the loudest voice in the room to be effective—I've found that real power often shows up in quiet leadership. I remember once, during a restaurant opening, there was chaos in the kitchen and panic in the air. Instead of yelling or commanding attention, I calmly pulled my team aside, reminded them of why we do what we do, and helped plate food myself until things settled. That moment reinforced what I believe: leadership isn't about noise—it's about presence, clarity, and heart. Power, for me, means influence without ego.

Owning my power has helped me lead with empathy. I don't need to prove myself by pretending to be someone else. I lead with my whole story—my roots, my mistakes, my culture, and my dreams. That authenticity allows me to make space for others to do the same.

I don't know if I had just one "calling" moment—but I know I've had many reminders. I realized the impact of simply showing up, of believing in someone when they don't yet believe in themselves. And sometimes, the impact isn't seen right away. These students are young; they don't always understand in the moment what your presence means. But over the years since I started teaching in 2010, many of them have returned—some with their own kids in tow—just to say thank you. They remember... They come back! And that, to me, is one of the greatest gifts of being an educator.

As a restaurateur, when a client approached me sometimes in tears, telling me that dining at our places reminded them of home, of their mother's cooking and the music they used to dance to together—these moments—small, profound, emotional—grounded me in my purpose. They didn't come with applause, but they filled me with the quiet certainty that I was exactly where I was meant to be.

I mentor and uplift other women by leading with transparency. I believe in financial and emotional independence. I talk openly about the messy parts of the journey, and I celebrate other women without competition. I want them to know they are allowed to want more—and go after it.

What do I hope others take from my story? That resilience doesn't mean you never struggle. It means you keep showing up anyway. You adapt. You rise. You push. And you do it with heart.

People often tell me they admire how feminine I am while still being strong and driven. I take pride in that. I've never seen softness as weakness. I learned that from my parents, from experience, and from becoming the kind of woman I needed to see growing up.

There's so much more I could say—about juggling motherhood and lesson plans, about the sacrifices of building a business, about the incredible (and exhausting) joy of being a Latina leader. But if there's one thing I've learned, it's this: being an ELLA PODEROSA doesn't mean you have it all figured out. It means you lead with love, with grit, and with the kind of joy that can only come from dancing salsa in your kitchen while folding laundry.

And yes—I still do that, too.

ADVICE THAT CHANGED MY LIFE

Set clear goals for yourself—both short-term and long-term—but don't get lost in the enormity of the journey. Big dreams often come with messy, unpredictable paths, and that's okay. Focus on taking consistent steps forward, no matter how small. Progress rarely looks perfect, but perseverance turns vision into reality.

Biography

Nivia Piña-Medina was born and raised in Puerto Rico, where her deep connection to culture, family, and tradition began. After moving to the mainland United States, she pursued her passion for science and education, earning a B.S. in Industrial Biotechnology from the University of Puerto Rico, a Master's in Biochemistry from Brandeis University, and a Master's in Education from the University of Massachusetts Boston. She is also a Howard Hughes Scholarship recipient and earned Girl Scout Silver and Gold Medals for leadership and community involvement.

Nivia began her career as a science teacher and special educator in Boston Public Schools before evolving into a restaurateur, community leader, wife, and mother. With her husband, Héctor Piña, she co-founded a restaurant group with over 40 years of combined culinary experience, including Merengue Restaurant, Vejigantes, Doña Habana, Merengue Express, and Vejigantes Downtown Worcester. Her restaurant concepts—especially Vejigantes—celebrate Puerto Rican heritage through food, design, and storytelling.

She has served as a Board Member of the Independent Professionals Association and Vice Chair of the Urban College Foundation. Through her food, advocacy, and leadership, Nivia brings the warmth, resilience, and identity of Puerto Rico to Boston's culinary and cultural landscape.

Nivia Piña-Medina

Instagram: @ninibella10

Facebook: Nivia Pina-Medina

RAIN COULDN'T WASH ME AWAY

ROSA MARIA SALAS

"You don't need to be born in power to rise in it—sometimes, you build it one tear and one triumph at a time."

DEDICATION

To my beautiful mother—your strength is my foundation, your love my shelter, your faith my light. You taught me grace through struggle and resilience through love. To my three incredible daughters, my reason to shine; to my husband, who has loved me faithfully for 37 years; to my precious grandkids, my joy; to my sisters and brothers, my first best friends; and to my Papi, who made us his own—I love you all.

That day, the sky was pouring. Our small apartment sat at the bottom of a hill, in what felt like the belly of the earth. Water rushed down toward our door like it knew where we were. I remember standing by the window, watching the rain snake past the walkway, swirling around the drain, as if the whole world was washing away. Inside, I cried—not just because I missed my mother, but because I could feel her pain. She was doing everything she could to raise three children under four years old while my biological father, though still her husband, was gone in every way that mattered.

She left us with a kind neighbor that day—a friend, a woman whose name I no longer remember but whose kindness I never forgot. I don't know if I was crying out of fear or hunger, or maybe just because I sensed that something was wrong. She gave me a piece of cuca bread to soothe me. That bread, in that moment, was love.

It was one of the first moments I realized how fragile life could be—but also how powerful love, community, and small acts of care could be. That rainy day etched itself into my spirit and became the beginning of a truth I would carry forever: I was not born with power, but I would rise into it.

As I grew, so did my understanding of survival. My mother, Eloina Figueroa Feliciano, despite every betrayal and burden, carried herself with resilience. She didn't wait for someone to save her. She worked, hustled, and made a way for us. Watching her, I learned early that strength isn't loud—it's silent. It's waking up every day and doing what needs to be done, even when your heart is breaking.

In 1970 we eventually moved back to the U.S., settling in New York City. Life there wasn't easy, but it was a new chapter— one that came with its own lessons. I didn't come from wealth or privilege. I came from working-class roots, where dreams were whispered in kitchens and chased between jobs and raising kids. I saw the struggle all around me. But I also saw perseverance, culture, laughter, and the importance of giving back.

When I was around four years old, I became aware—really aware—of my mother's daily struggles. She was trying to make a new life for us in the city we now called home. She needed childcare to be able to work, and I could sense the weight she carried, even at that young age. We lived on Pitt Street, in a one-bedroom apartment on the fifth floor. The ceilings were high—I remember staring up at them in wonder—and the bedroom was large enough to fit two big beds. My mother and I shared one, while my sister Carmen and brother Nelson shared the other.

Though we didn't have much, I never remember feeling unloved. My mother was strict, yes, but there was never a doubt in my heart that she loved us fiercely. She worked tirelessly every single day. And despite having little money and no help, she always managed to put food on the table. We may not have had much, but she gave us everything.

When I was about five, a new light entered our lives—my Papi. That's what I've always called him, because he became the father our biological one never was. My mom met Efrain Torres, a tall, handsome, hard-working young man who fell in love not just with my mother, but with all of us. I'll never forget the way he looked at her—with admiration, respect, and love. And he embraced us as his own without hesitation.

That year, for my fifth birthday, my Mami threw me a little party, and Papi gave me a beautiful gold cross necklace. It may seem like a small gesture, but I remember it like it was yesterday. How many people can say they remember their fifth birthday gift in such detail? That necklace wasn't just a piece of jewelry—it was a symbol of love, of being chosen, of being seen.

Eventually, my mami and papi moved in together, and just like that, we became a family. They later had two more children together—my baby sister, Laura, and my baby brother, Efrain. I still call them that to this day. And though most people wouldn't know that Papi wasn't our biological father, it never mattered. We already had his last name. What mattered was that he showed up. He stayed. He loved.

I constantly watched my Mami hustle. Though she became a stay-at-home mom raising five children, she still found a way to become an entrepreneur. Everyone in our neighborhood knew her—every block was another stop to talk business. She always had a side hustle, whether it was crocheting, sewing, or crafting something unique to help make ends meet. Mami had a magic touch.

She would create handmade crib sets for new mothers, complete with elaborate hand-painted designs, or crochet delicate dresses for newborn girls. Hats, booties, even stunning custom-made curtains—she did it all. To this day, I still don't know how she found the time. Maybe it was while we were at school, but somehow, she made it work.

People would bring her their ideas, and she'd bring them to life—beautiful curtains in every size and color, full of character and charm. If someone hadn't paid in full, they didn't get their items. And if they had only made a partial payment, guess who she sent to collect the rest? My brother Nelson and I. We'd knock on doors with clear instructions: "No money, give back the curtain."

That experience taught me the value of hard work and money. My mami worked tirelessly, and her earnings helped keep our household afloat. More than that, it gave me a sense of responsibility at a young age.

As a child, you don't always recognize the sacrifices your parents make. It's only when you become an adult yourself that you see it clearly. My mami was fully dedicated to us. She fought for us, never gave up, and never stopped loving us with everything she had.

She is the very definition of resilience.

I graduated from high school in 1985 and enrolled at Borough of Manhattan Community College, where I studied for two years. During that time, I found myself in a very difficult and painful relationship—not with a man, but with a boy who only pretended to be one. He was emotionally abusive and deeply hurtful.

Like so many women, I didn't know how to leave. I felt stuck, ashamed, and afraid. It was an incredibly challenging time in my young life. Deep down, I knew my mami would be heartbroken if she ever found out how he was treating me.

He entered my life as someone charming and kind, but within a few months, his true colors emerged. The control, the manipulation, the cruelty—it all slowly took over until I could barely recognize myself.

It wasn't until the tragic death of my nephew that something inside me shifted. That heartbreaking loss gave me the strength I needed to walk away. In the midst of my grief, I finally saw my worth and knew I deserved more. Leaving him was one of the most defining—and most important—decisions I ever made.

I moved to Webster, Massachusetts, to be closer to my sister Carmen, my brother-in-law Edwin, and their beautiful daughter Cecilie, after they had lost their son. It was a much-needed escape from the toxic relationship that had plagued my young life and left me living in fear.

Moving to Webster was a fresh start—a chance to step away from the fast-paced chaos of the city and embrace a quieter, more peaceful way of life. It wasn't just a change of scenery; it was a turning point.

We all made the decision to move to Worcester—a vibrant city that has since become my home for over thirty+ years. Worcester brought with it new energy and a renewed sense of purpose. It was where my real journey began.

I quickly found work at a bank and began building my professional path. I worked my way up in the banking industry, dedicating over 15 years to that career. It was during those years that I began to find my footing—not just financially, but personally and professionally—as I continued to rebuild my life on my own terms.

I first met my husband, German, in 1984 at a party that would change the course of my life. There was an instant spark between us, the kind of connection that feels both surprising and familiar all at once. We dated briefly, but distance got in the way, and for a while, our paths went in different directions.

Years later, when I moved back to Worcester, fate brought us together again. This time, the timing was right — it felt like life had been quietly preparing us for this second chance. German and I married in 1988, and from there, we built a life filled with love, laughter, and family. Together we welcomed three beautiful daughters — Amanda Eloie, Aurea Mari, and Jasmeen Lydia — each a reflection of the love story that began all those years ago at a simple party.

They are now my "WHY." They are my strength and my

motivation to make a difference and to never give up. They've seen me work my tail off, going back to school, and continue learning even after raising them to be strong and resilient.

Worcester is where I raised my daughters, built my career, and truly found my voice. My path wasn't straight. I didn't wake up one day and decide to become a leader. It happened one moment at a time—starting when I took a job at a nonprofit helping first-time homebuyers and foreclosure prevention. I was there to teach financial literacy, helping educate families on buying their first home and helping those who were in foreclosure. What I discovered was how much people were hurting, how much they just needed someone to believe in them.

I saw myself in so many of those clients—single mothers, immigrants, women of color navigating systems that were never designed for us. Every time I sat across the table from one of them, I remembered my mother. I remembered being hungry, cold, scared—and being given a piece of cuca bread by a neighbor who cared. And so, I chose to be that neighbor for someone else, again, and again.

Over time, my work in housing and financial advocacy became a calling. I wasn't just helping people fill out forms—I was helping them reclaim their dignity, their voice, their stability. That work led me to leadership roles, to boardrooms, to roundtables where decisions were made. Sometimes, I was the only Latina in the room. Often, I was underestimated. But I no longer cried in silence—I spoke up. I advocated for inclusion. I used every table I sat at to pull up more chairs.

Being on the board of a nonprofit has been deeply rewarding. My journey began in 2001 with a nonprofit called **Centro Las Americas,** an organization that was dedicated to helping individuals and families Achieve self-sufficiency and build purposeful lives. Later, I became involved with **Adelante Worcester,** an organization very close to my heart. Their mission to promote and empower the Hispanic/ Latino community of Greater Worcester resonated deeply with me. Through networking, professional development, and cultural events, Adelante helps bring people together, amplify Latino voices, and strengthen community leadership. I've been proud to be part of this work since 2009.

When my best friend, Elizabeth Cruz, asked me to join the Latin American Business Organization (LABO) board, I felt an immediate connection. My mother was a self-made entrepreneur, and she never had access to the tools and resources that LABO now offers. Joining that board was an act of love—and legacy.

In 2023, I became one of the Founding Board Members and Treasurer (now Vice President) of ELLA—Empowering Latina Leaders Affirmation—alongside Elizabeth Cruz. ELLA was born out of fire, faith, and the sisterhood that Elizabeth Cruz brought to life. A movement rooted in the belief that when one woman rises, she lifts others with her. Through workshops, summits, and community initiatives, we have created a powerful network of *mujeres* (women) who lead with courage, grace, and unapologetic purpose.

I look back on that little girl in the rain often. I cry for her sometimes. But more often, I thank her—because she never gave up. She kept believing. She held on long enough to become the woman I am today.

My *mamita* had everything to do with who I am now—as a mother, daughter, and person. I see myself continuing this work—for the love of my *familia* and for *mi bella madre* (my beautiful mother). I want not only for my life to be meaningful, but for my daughters to see meaning in my life.

I am the daughter of a powerful Boricua mother.

I am a wife, a mother, a grandmother, a community warrior, and a proud ELLA PODEROSA.

I walk through doors with purpose—and I make damn sure I leave them open behind me.

ADVICE THAT CHANGED MY LIFE

The best piece of advice I've ever received came from my mother:

"Nunca bajes la cabeza. Si tropiezas, levántate con dignidad." ("Never lower your head. If you stumble, rise with dignity.")

She taught me that strength is not in how loud you are but in how fiercely you rise after every fall. That advice carried me through moments when I felt invisible, unheard, or overlooked. It reminded me to lead with pride, even when I was hurting, and to never let anyone make me feel small.

One piece of advice I now offer others is this: Don't wait for the world to give you permission. Create your own table, bring your own chair, and speak your truth— even if your voice shakes. For too long, I waited for others to validate me, to see me. Now, I walk with the knowledge that my lived experience, my voice, and my leadership are enough.

Biography

Rosa Maria Salas is a proud Puerto Rican, a devoted daughter, sister, wife and mother. Married for 37 years, a loving mother to three beautiful daughters—Amanda, Aurea, and Jasmeen—and proud grandmother to five grandchildren, two wonderful boys and three equally beautiful girls. She is deeply committed to building bridges of opportunity and leaving doors open for the next generation of leaders. Born in Bridgeport, Connecticut, and raised in New York City, Rosa Maria has spent over three decades in Worcester, Massachusetts, before relocating to Danielson, Connecticut, in 2020.

She is a passionate and dynamic community leader with over 25 years of experience in the mortgage and real estate industry. During a pivotal chapter in her life, her career began in the nonprofit sector, where she educated first-time homebuyers and advocated for foreclosure prevention—work that ignited her lifelong mission to promote financial empowerment and equity.

Rosa Maria proudly serves as the Vice President and Founding Board Member of Empowering Latina Leaders Affirmation (ELLA). She is also the Vice President of Adelante Worcester and Secretary of the Latin American Business Organization (LABO), where she actively champions Latino voices and economic growth within her community.

Rosa Maria Salas

rmsalas.graaj@gmail.com
LinkedIn: https://www.linkedin.com/in/rosamariasalas/
Facebook: https://www.facebook.com/rmsalas1
Instagram: @graaj1966

GIVING UP IS NOT AN OPTION

VIANEY GODOY

"Today, I don't just clean spaces; I transform lives, because when a woman moves forward, her family and her community move forward with her."

DEDICATION

A mi madre, María Toñita.

Mujer valiente, incansable y llena de amor.

Tu vida fue mi primera lección de fuerza, de dignidad y de fe.

Todo lo que he logrado, todo lo que soy, lleva tu nombre en silencio.

Gracias por enseñarme a no rendirme, incluso cuando el camino dolía.

Este capítulo es mi manera de abrazarte con palabras,
y de decirte que tu sacrificio nunca fue en vano.
Te amo con todo mi corazón, mamá.

I remember my hometown, Tiucal, Guatemala, with great affection, as well as Asunción Mita—places that shaped my story and identity. In Asunción Mita, I lived in a loving neighborhood where I grew close to my neighbors: Mrs. Celia, Mrs. Gela, Mrs. Sole, and my beloved godmother Luisa, who is now in heaven but left a lasting mark on my childhood with her tenderness, thoughtful gestures, and the cakes she made for my birthdays.

We returned to Tiucal so my mother could take care of her sisters after my *abuelita* Blanca passed away. Her death left a big void not only in our hearts, but in the lives of her young daughters who still needed guidance and love. My mother, the oldest sibling, stepped in with quiet strength and took on the role of caregiver without hesitation. It was an act of deep love and sacrifice; she put her own plans on hold to support her family. Watching her raise her sisters while caring for her own children showed me what true resilience and devotion look like. Her selflessness left a lasting impression on me that I carry to this day.

I also have fond memories of a small village called La Playa, known for its beautiful lagoon. It was a special place where I shared meaningful moments with my family. We were able to settle there, thanks to a close friend of my father, who later became my father-in-law. I'm also grateful to Mrs. Judith, my mother-in-law, who supported us during that time, never imagining that one day her son and I would build a life together. My husband Belter and I lost touch as children, but life brought us back together years later, here in this country the United states.

I am the oldest sibling among four brothers, Jerardo, Enio, Juanfer, and Jose whom I love with all my heart. I've always strived to be a good example for them. My childhood was shaped by both the love and struggles of my parents. My father worked hard at a government-run irrigation company for agricultural plantations in Guatemala, but he had to leave due to delayed payments, a common issue in many small towns. He also faced internal battles, and, although his struggle with alcoholism affected us deeply, I have long since forgiven him. I still love and respect him for the good he tried to do.

However, inside our home, the violence caused by his alcoholism left deep emotional scars. I remember the fear in my mother's eyes—a strong and silent woman who, despite everything, never stopped fighting. As a child, I felt helpless, wishing I could change our situation but not knowing how.

My mother Maria Antonia Guevara was the strength that held our family together. She raised us and cared for her sisters with tireless love and dedication. Her example of sacrifice and service continues to guide me. She taught me that helping others, caring, and giving our best is an act of love that always brings blessings in return.

Today, thanks to God, I can proudly say I fulfilled my promise to build a different kind of home. My husband is a responsible and loving man. Our home is free of alcohol, and my children Jeffrey and Jasmin Gonzalez Godoy have never known the fear or instability I once lived through. They are growing up in a space filled with love, respect, and safety.

I've learned that it is possible to change the course of our lives. No matter how difficult our childhood was or what obstacles we face, if we trust in God and ourselves and if we work hard and stay determined we can write a new story.

When I first arrived in Boston eighteen years ago in 2007 for a better life. Everything felt overwhelming—the cold weather, the language barrier, and the fast rhythm of life. I started working in restaurants, cleaning kitchens late at night and serving tables during the day. I remember coming home exhausted, my hands dry from cleaning products, but my heart full of determination. I kept telling myself that one day I would have my own company, a place where women like me could feel safe and respected.

Despite the challenges I faced in my country, Boston has become a place of opportunity for me. It hasn't been easy, but through hard work and perseverance, I built a cleaning company that provides dignified employment for women.

This company didn't grow overnight. I learned early on that asking for help is a strength, not a weakness. I was never afraid to seek guidance, apply for grants, or reach out for mentorship. I constantly looked for programs and people who could help me grow, not just as a business owner, but as a leader. I knocked on doors, attended workshops, filled out countless applications, and took advantage of every opportunity to learn and expand. Each time I asked for help or applied for something, I gained new insights and tools.

That persistence opened doors for me. It was my sacrifice, my commitment to always do my work with excellence, and the courage to ask for help that made the difference. I knocked on many doors, asking questions everywhere I could–even to other businesses that had nothing to do with mine. Through that journey, I met incredible organizations like **North Shore Latino, ALX, Entrepreneurs Forever, and ELLA,** all which became essential parts of my business growth. Resources and connections I never imagined possible. Because of those efforts, my company has grown, served more families, and become a source of empowerment for other women. I truly believe that when women support each other, we all rise together.

I am especially grateful to the **Spanish group of Entrepreneurs Forever here in Boston** and to two wonderful people who have guided and supported me with so much kindness and wisdom–**Leonela Gonzalez and Kevin Moforte.** Their encouragement and belief in me have helped me take important steps forward, and I will always carry that gratitude with me.

During these training sessions for small business owners, I also met **Maria Gonzalez,** an exceptional woman who has helped me face challenges and overcome them. She has guided me to finding the certifications my business needs.

This business is more than a source of income. It's a space where women feel seen, valued, and supported, a place where they can build better futures for themselves and their families. By lifting one another up, we transform not only our own lives but also our communities. That legacy inspires me every single day to keep moving forward.

ADVICE THAT CHANGED MY LIFE

Life isn't always easy. Sometimes it presents challenges that seem impossible to overcome. But I've learned that those challenges aren't walls, they're steps that help us grow. Every difficulty taught me something: patience, inner strength, the importance of family, and the power of never giving up.

The best advice I ever received came from my mother. She used to tell me, *"No matter how hard life gets, never stop moving forward. Even when you feel like you have nothing left, walk–because every small step is still progress."*

At the time, I didn't fully understand her words. But as I grew older and faced my own struggles–leaving my country, and building a business from scratch–I realized she had given me the strength that shaped my life.

There were moments when I felt lost and afraid, when everything seemed too heavy to carry. But I remembered her voice. I remembered how she sacrificed for our family, how she kept going even when life was cruel. Her advice taught me that faith and perseverance can turn pain into purpose.

Now every time I feel tired, I remind myself of her words. They became my foundation–the reason I never gave and the reason I now tell other women *"You can do it too."*

I want you to know that no matter where you come from or how big your obstacles may seem, there is always hope. There is always light at the end of the tunnel. When we choose to rewrite our story with faith and hard work, we create a legacy that transcends generations.

Today, I can look back and say with pride: every sacrifice was worth it, because I built a home where love and peace reign. If I can do it, so can you. Trust yourself, believe in your abilities, and never stop dreaming.

Remember, your story matters. Your efforts count. And with perseverance and an open heart, you can transform your life and the lives of those you love.

Biography

Vianey Godoy, a Latina entrepreneur and founder of Godoy Cleaning Corporation, arrived in the United States from Guatemala 20 years ago in South Carolina, and 2 years later to Boston with a dream and the determination to make it come true. From working alone cleaning houses, she went on to lead a team of women, many of them single mothers, to whom she offers dignified opportunities and flexible schedules so they can be present for their children.

Her company earned Massachusetts' MWBE diverse supplier certification, unlocking larger-scale opportunities and reinforcing her dedication to delivering safe, professional, and top-quality service.

Vianey has turned her company into a source of employment, quality, and hope, proving that with effort, discipline, and heart, dreams do come true.

Vianey Godoy
godoycleaning82@icloud.com
godoycleaningcorp.com
Instagram: @godoycleaning1

About The Author

Elizabeth Cruz is the Founder and President of Empowering Latina Leaders Affirmation (ELLA) and the President of the Latin American Business Organization (LABO). She also serves as a steering committee member of *Unidos in Power*, amplifying her advocacy for representation, equity, and community empowerment. Through LABO, she leads a full business development center that supports entrepreneurs of all backgrounds—men and women alike—helping them start, grow, and sustain their businesses with education, certification, and advocacy.

With a degree in computer science and more than 20 years of experience in information technology, consulting, and real estate, Elizabeth blends technical expertise with business strategy and a steadfast commitment to empowerment. Her journey—from being the only Latina and woman in her computer science classes to becoming an IT consultant, real estate strategist, and community leader—shaped her mission to open doors for others and change the narrative of what leadership looks like for Latinas. She is guided by her quote: *Great leaders don't close the door behind them.*

Elizabeth is also a creative voice, writing poetry, songs, and stories that reflect resilience, faith, and cultural pride. She is a contributing author in Hispanic Star Rising Volume IV, further amplifying her voice and commitment to storytelling as a tool for empowerment.

Through ELLA, she has created a safe space where Latinas can see themselves reflected in leadership, mentor one another, and rise collectively. Beyond her visionary leadership, she has helped over 600 families build generational wealth through real estate.

A proud wife, mother, and storyteller, songwriter, Elizabeth carries her mother's legacy of love, resilience, and gratitude into every room, every conversation, and every life she touches.

Elizabeth Cruz has been widely recognized for her leadership, community impact, and professional excellence. In 2024, she was honored with the **ALX100 Award,** the **United Way Women's Initiative Lois B. Green Leadership Award,** and named among **Worcester Business Journal's Power 100.** Previously, she was also celebrated as one of the **Outstanding Women in Business** (2022). In real estate, Elizabeth's commitment to excellence earned her recognition from **Keller Williams Realty as a Million Dollar Club member (2019)** and ranked **#3 in Sold Listing Volume and #5 in Closed Sales Volume (2020).**

Elizabeth Cruz

liz.reinasincorona@gmail.com
https://www.linkedin.com/in/ecdejesus/
https://www.instagram.com/liz_reinasincorona/

Made in the USA
Middletown, DE
06 January 2026

24397303R00141